THE GENERAL THEORY OF ECONOMIC EFFICIENCY

Volume 1
First Edition

By
Stephan H. Loh

SHL Resources Inc.

The General Theory of Economic Efficiency

Volume 1
First Edition

Copyright © Stephan Hsiao Loh, 1999
First Published in 1999

Published by:
SHL Resources Inc.
1603 Waterford Road
Yardley, PA 19067

Library of Congress Catalog Card Number: 99-96960

Loh, Stephan H.
The General Theory of Economic Efficiency
1. Title. 2 Economic theory. 3. Value theory 4. Price theory. 5. Economic Efficiency. 6. Optimal economic parameters. 7. Economic methodology. 8. Productivity and growth.

ISBN: 0-9673668-0-1

Printed in the USA by
Morris Publishing
3212 East Highway 30 • Kearney, NE 68847 • 1 800-650-7888

Contents

PREFACE

This book is intended for all readers who are interested in the most recent breakthrough in economic theory. I consider this book a must-read for all economists and economic policy makers. It may be used as a text book for college-level economic courses or supplemental reading material for students who major in economics. Readers do not need to have an economic background to read this book.

In the past 100 years, economists have used more and more mathematics in economic research, less and less traditional substance of classic economics. Flipping through economic journals today, we find more and more fancy economic equations, but less discussion about the supporting economic principles that are employed by economists to create those equations. To address this, I decided to go back to the root of economic inquiry. The very foundation of economics is the theory of exchange value. It is the very basic economic question that economists and philosophers have asked themselves since the beginning of time. There are two major schools of economic thought on value theory. One is the classic labor theory of value; the other is the marginalist theory of value. The classic labor theory of value failed to correctly theorize concerning the profit and interest. While the marginal theory of value seems to be universally correct, I have found and seek to prove in this book that it is totally incorrect at its root. That marginal utility equals price is regarded as the basic conclusion of the marginal theory of value. However, I argue in this book that they are not equal. The marginalist believes that price is determined by marginal utility. The higher the marginal utility is, the higher the price. I argue in this book that higher marginal utility could actually result in lower prices. This book has created a new theory of value; in writing it, I introduce a brand new theoretical approach to economics. This will create a paradigm shift in the 21st century in economic thinking. This book is a revolution in the theory of value. It is the next step in the evolving field of economic theory. In 1776, Adam Smith published "An Inquiry into the Nature and Causes of the Wealth of Nations." In his book, Adam Smith established the classic labor theory of value. In the 1870s, William Stanley Jevons started the marginalist revolution in the theory of value by publishing his work "The Theory of

Political Economy." In 1999, I present this book "The General Theory of Economic Efficiency" to start another revolution in the theory of value.

Economics is the study on how to efficiently allocate economic resources. One important aim of this study is to link economic parameters to economic efficiency. In doing so, I discover the optimal economic parameters of a market economic system.

"The General Theory of Economic Efficiency" is a three volume book set. This is volume 1 of a planned three-book project. In the first volume, I introduce the labor theory of value in the first chapter; the optimal economic operating parameters in ideal economy, such as optimal interest rate and optimal profit rate in the second chapter; optimal economic parameters for an imperfect world in the third chapter; and how the reality works when compared with the optimal economic parameter in the fourth chapter, where I will explain a list of classic economic paradoxes, which have puzzled economists for centuries.

Volume Two and Volume Three will deal with other major economic issues, such as inflation rate, international trade, exchange rate, land use, taxation, unemployment, and economic recession. The writing plan is subject to change.

I owe a great deal to many people who helped and encouraged me in writing this book. I would like to thank the following editors for their assistance and contribution to the writing. Rachael Brooke Ryan edited the first chapter. Tara Sanchez edited the First, third, fourth chapter, appendix, part of introduction, and made valuable recommendations to the structure of the first chapter. Her recommendation made the first chapter much easy to understand. Mare Adams Fallon edited the entire manuscript, corrected many hard to find errors. Copy editor, Monica LoRusso edited the preface, introduction, Chapter One and Two. Kathe Martin edited the preface and introduction. Sherry Roberts edited the back cover text. I am grateful to librarians at many libraries. Special thanks to librarians at Federal Reserve Bank of Philadelphia. I appreciate Henry H. Gu for reading the manuscript. He made several suggestions that improved the book. I would like to thank my wife Zheng Yuan, for her encouragement, patience, love, understanding, tolerance, and my parents for their assistance in getting readers' feedback.

Introduction

As the title of the book suggests, this is a study of economic efficiency. The theory of economic efficiency is based on the theory of value. An economy runs like an engine in an automobile; many components work together. Economists study market economy by observing the key parameters of an economy, such as inflation, productivity growth rate, and profit rate. Many of the parameters of the economy have a lot to do with the efficiency of the market economic system. In advanced automobile engineering, the operating parameters are controlled by a computer, which measures parameters of the engine. The objective of such an engine control system is to improve fuel efficiency, reduce pollution, and produce maximum power when needed. Automobile engineers have discovered relationships between the objectives they try to achieve and the parameters of the engine, such as ignition timing, fuel pressure, fuel and air-mixing ratio, and so forth. A market economy is similar in this regard. It has economic parameters. Economists and politicians have some common objectives. These objectives are efficiency, environmental friendliness, fast economic development, stability and full employment. This book will explore the optimal relationships between some economic parameters when we are trying to achieve maximum economic efficiency.

The major parameters I will explore in the first volume include inflation rate, profit rate, productivity improvement rate, and average compensation increase rate. As a by-product of the study, I will also answer questions that have been raised by economists in the past challenging the validity of labor value theory. Thus, I will also address paradoxes like: (1) Why diamonds have very high exchange value when they contain little labor value, and (2) Why old wine is more expensive when it takes the same amount of labor to produce.

There are many reasons why you may want to read this book. Economists, particularly those who teach economics courses, will want to know the latest shocking discovery in economic thinking, and want to be the first to know the latest economic breakthrough in the theory of value since Adam Smith and the marginalist revolution. Economic Professors do not want to be viewed as ignorant when their students have read this book while they have not. The smartest economists want to use the thinking in this book to advance their careers and help them to advance the research in which they are interested. Students will want to know the limitations of mainstream economics, will want to view the evolving world of economics from a new and different angle with a new and different philosophy, and will want to be known as the smartest guy among classmates and friends. For the average person, you want to know how the economy operates; how it can be more efficient. Most importantly, you want to know how it may affect your life, your money, and your investment if government officials and center bank economists accept this new economic thinking.

The methodology used in this book is quite different from that of mainstream economics. Many mainstream economists argue that economics deals with what we can observe, not with what ought to be. I, however, deal with what ought to be. The whole theme of this work is based on what ought to be in an economy, which is more efficient. It ought to operate consistently at its peak optimal performance level.

When automobile engineers try to maximize fuel efficiency, they put the specific engine through tests to find out the relationships among speed, fuel consumption, and other operating parameters such as intake air speed, air and fuel-mix ratio. Then, the engineers construct a mathematical model and use it to build the computer that controls the engine. The mathematical model the engineers built is not theory; it is an engineering mathematical model for a specific engine. For a discovery to become a theory, it has to have a universal validity in a predefined domain. This domain may not have a time limit or geographic limit. When economists produce a mathematical model that simulates hundreds of U.S. economic parameters based on past U.S. economic observations, the mathematical model is not a theory. It is an engineering modeling of economic phenomenon. It is not a theory since it cannot predict into the future without a time limit and country limit. For example, a model of such kind may be able to predict economic phenomenon only from 1960 to 1990. It cannot predict anything from 1991 and beyond. Nor can it be used to predict other market economies, such as Russia's economy or the Japanese economy. An economic theory must be universally applicable. An economic explanation and prediction can become an economic theory if it can explain phenomena of all market economies without limitations on which country it can apply to, if it can make predictions that do not have to be restricted to a specific year or decade.

There is a difference in testability between engineering mathematical models and theory. When automobile engineers build a mathematical model to predict the relationships among an engine's operating parameter and its output, the engineers expect the mathematical model to reflect the average situation. In other words, deviation is expected due to inconsistency in manufacturing. For example, if the mathematical model predicts the power of the engine will increase 10% when the pressures of intake air increase 20%, then it is expected that every engine tested will perform somewhat differently. One engine may produce an 11% power increase with a 20% increase in the intake air pressure, while another engine tested may produce only a 9% power increase under the same condition. Those manufacturing-related deviations do not falsify the mathematical model the engineers used to build the engine control system.

When economists build a mathematical model in an attempt to predict the change in an economy of a specific country, they are building an engineering mathematical model similar to what the auto engineers build to predict the engine output, input and operating parameters. The economic mathematical model usually is useful for a specific country and period of time. Similarly, the auto engineering mathematical model is useful for only that specific brand and model of engine. In an economic mathematical model, error of prediction is the norm, since the basic principle of the economic mathematical modeling is an averaging statistical process, the objective of which is to produce a curve to fit all the data concerned. A methodology of such kind voids any falsification. Some economists even proudly announce that the contradiction between reality and their economic model can in no way falsify their economic mathematical model. Discounting reality has traditionally been a necessary condition for economic modeling to exist. Economic mathematical modeling is useful to economic policymakers and economists, especially when economists are unable to produce any alternative solid economic theory. But regardless of how useful the economic mathematical model can be, it is not in any way an economic theory. For a body of thought to become an economic theory, it must stand up to reality checks and tests of falsification.

In the second chapter, we discuss an ideal economy. From the analysis of ideal economy, we will discover the relations among many important economic parameters, such as profit rate, inflation rate, and productivity improvement rate of the economy. One may wonder what an imagined ideal economy has to do with economics and economy. Think about Newton's Three Laws of Motion, which are a set of basic laws in physics. Newton's three laws, just like the economic relations I discovered in the second chapter, only work in ideal conditions. For example, Newton's first law of motion states that if the forces on an object equal zero, then the object will remain moving at constant velocity or stay at rest. This relation only exists in highly ideal conditions. In reality, the objects we observe daily are subject to friction, resistance, gravity and many other forces. For example, a car will eventually stop if we stop giving gasoline to the engine. Objects on earth are subject to gravitational force. Just like the three laws of motion Newton discovered, the law of economics also describes relations among parameters in ideal or unrealistic conditions.

The third chapter will discuss optimal parameters for the real world economy. These parameters are based on ideal economic conditions that the real world economy does not experience, therefore it will be necessary to modify the conclusion of the second chapter in order to obtain a set of optimal parameters that can be used in the real world. This will require taking into consideration the complicating factors that were set aside in Chapter Two. During this process, a wage compensator is introduced into the equations.

We will discuss reasons why the U.S. economy showed faster economic growth in the 1960s than in the 1980s and 1990s. Applying the Law of Optimal Parameters for the Real World Economy to U.S. economic statistics suggests that the U.S. productivity growth rate could have been 216% higher if the U.S. economic parameters were set to the Optimal Parameters. The result also suggests that the world economic growth rate could be much higher if all market economies apply this law.

Chapter Four discusses how market forces, or the "invisible hand", work in terms of moving the real world economy toward the ideal economy, and the limitations of the market mechanism. Understanding the defects of the market is crucial to economic policymakers and economists alike. Explanations of famous economic paradoxes and application examples are presented at the end of the chapter.

To make it easy to read through this book, I recommend the first time readers to skip the Market Model 7 - 13 in Chapter One (Page 55-86) and page 136-152 in Chapter Two.

CHAPTER 1

THE THEORY OF VALUE

METHODOLOGY

TWO TYPES OF ECONOMIST

There are two types of economists. The first type studies economics from a distance and does not get involved in policy making. These economists ask how the economy works in order to learn how to predict changes. They use descriptive language and fancy mathematical functions to describe the relationships between economic variables. They believe that the market system is naturally perfect and self-adjusting, such that human intervention is unnecessary and government intervention is undesirable. The market system will work things out on its own if given enough time. Most importantly, these economists believe that real world economic data cannot be used to disprove economic theory. Any contradiction between their theory and real world events is considered insignificant and is ignored. Their economic theory is merely a mathematical game of thought. Today, many economists are involved in mathematical modeling based on economic statistics. Mathematical modeling by its nature is a process to produce a curve or a function that best fits the data used for the modeling. Many economists even believe mathematical modeling is the way to do economic theoretical research. There are three problems with mathematical modeling. First, the curve or function produced by mathematical modeling cannot make all data fit perfectly. The errors between the curve (function) and reality is perfectly normal for this kind of research methodology. This is why statistical technique is heavily used to reduce overall error. Since the error between the curve and the reality is expected, it makes no sense to falsify the "theory." Since the mathematical modeling cannot be falsified, it should not be called "theory." I suggest it be called "engineering modeling of economy" in order to distinguish it from "economic theory." Second, theory must be universally applicable in its defined domain. For example, if a theory is for market economy, it should be applicable to all market economies regardless of geographical location, type of government, race of its people, and time. Mathematical modeling, however, cannot meet these requirements. It is therefore, not theory, but "engineering modeling of economy." Third, the approach many economists take to do theoretical research by means of mathematical modeling puts the carriage before the horse. However, mathematical modeling of economy as a method for economic empirical research is valid and useful. It is one of many powerful tools widely used for empirical research.

In contrast, the second type of economist believes that economic theory and research should attempt to solve real world economic problems. These economists ask how the economy should work so that it can best serve human needs. Policy is clearly at the heart of this approach. The market system is believed to be basically good, but with some imperfections. Economists must identify these imperfections and prescribe corrective policy. Thus, these economists naturally believe that government intervention in the market system based on sound economic theory is not only desirable, but necessary. These economists also believe that any contradiction between economic theory and real world events is strong indication that one or more logical mistakes exist in the theory, and since the theory serves as a base for policy making, it must be tested by real world events. Unlike the first type, however, the second type of economist believes that economic theory is falsified when contradictory real world events are observed.

I am an economist of the second type, and this book is rooted in that philosophy. The first chapter examines how the market works; the second and third chapters examine how it should work; the fourth chapter discusses the reality of the market economy when compared with ideal operating conditions. Of course, there are many economists who fall somewhere in between the two types of economists.

TWO KINDS OF RESEARCHES

"The General Theory of Economic Efficiency" is a theory. What is the difference between this theory and many other mainstream "theories" built on mathematical modeling of economy? Table 1.1 summaries the difference between empirical research and theoretical research in economics. The empirical research method listed in this table is the method used by most economists today. However, some economists do not actually understand that although mathematical modeling is an extremely useful tool, it is not the way to do theoretical research. Empirical research is good at answering questions, such as "How much will investment spending change if the interest rate decreases 1/4%?" and, "If the average income level in area X increase by 500%, what will happen to the birth rate?"

Table 1. 1

	Empirical Research	Theoretical Research
Typical Method	Mathematical Modeling	Deduction based on a set of assumptions
Empirical Data	Needed to build the model	Not used directly
Falsification	Real world evidence cannot be used to disprove a "theory"-- Model	Real world evidence can be used to disprove an economic theory
Which is better?	One mathematical modeling is better than the other if it can make more accurate prediction	One economic theory is better than the other if it can stand real world test, and has wider range of applications
Evolution of the "theory"	Improvement can be made by improved function, more variables, more data, better mathematical technique	Change the assumptions of the theory, correct logical errors in deduction
Conclusion =	Logic (model, data)	Logic (assumptions, variables)
Application Domain	Time and country constraints	No time or country constraints

However, other questions are best answered by theoretical research, such as "How should a central bank set the interest rate so that the economy can operate at its peak efficiency?" and "What is optimal profit rate?" Empirical research and theoretical research typically use different research methodologies. For empirical research economists, mathematical modeling is the primary tool. The following example illustrates how mathematical modeling works. Suppose an economist collected the following data for the U.S. during the years 1990 - 1997, as shown in Table 1.2. It seems there is a linear relationship between the money supply increase rate and the GDP growth rate. The economist plots the data on a chart shown in Figure 1.1. (All data used here are hypothetical.) By applying statistical method, the economist found the linear function that best fits into the given data.

Table 1. 2

Year	Money supply Increase rate	GDP growth rate
1990	3%	1%
1991	5%	1.2%
1992	8%	2%
1993	12%	2.2%
1994	6%	2%
1995	15%	2.1%
1996	18%	2.2%
1997	12%	1.8%

The function is a straight line, as is shown in Figure 1.1. The black dots are the data points. Suppose a linear function is the best approximation to the given data, and the linear function is:

$$Y = 1.85 \times X \quad (1.1)$$

Where:
Y: GDP growth rate
X: Money supply growth rate

If we use any one pair of the given data to test how the linear function predicts the GDP growth rate, we will find that the prediction has frequent errors. For example, if $X = 8\%$, how much is Y? Applying the linear equation, we have:

$$Y = 0.185 \times 8\% = 1.48\%$$

However, the given data shows that in 1992 when $X = 8\%$, the GDP growth rate $Y = 2\%$. From this example, we see that the method of mathematical modeling guarantees error between the prediction and real data. Therefore, it is not possible to use any real world evidence to disprove the model. Furthermore, we cannot arbitrarily tell an economist using this model, let's call him Dr. Miller, that his model is invalid because it has 5% standard deviation. Dr. Miller will argue allowable standard

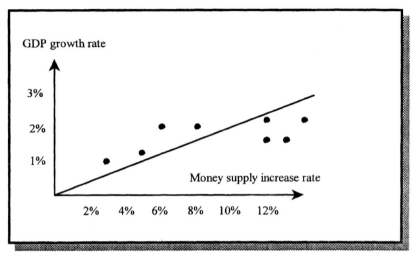

Figure 1.1

error should be 20%. We see from here that we have no way of winning this kind of argument, because how much error is okay is a value judgement, not a science. This is why we say the mathematical model of economy is cannot be falsified. This is why economists can proudly claim real word evidence cannot be used to disprove their "theories."

On the other side, theoretical economics can be falsified. Real world evidence can be used to disprove an economic theory.

The mathematical modeling of economy and economic theory evolve in different courses. To improve mathematical modeling, economists often rebuild their mathematical model. For example, in the above model, we use the change in money supply to predict the growth of GDP. To improve the model, we can incorporate more variables, such as interest rate, inflation, technology change, crude oil price change, education level change, spending change, and consumption change. Instead of a linear model, we can use more complex mathematical operations, such as square, square root, and differential equations. Instead of 8 years of economic statistical data, we can include 50 years of data. As we can see, the model becomes increasingly complex; it often requires huge computers to compute parameters and results.

When there is real world evidence that disproves an economic theory, it is time for economists to rethink their assumptions or the logic process upon which their theory is based. Improvement is often made by changing assumptions of the theory, and correcting errors in deduction.

$$\text{Conclusion} = \text{logic (model, data)} \qquad (1.2)$$

The conclusion we can obtain from a research method is determined before we see the conclusion. For empirical research, in this equation (1.2), the "conclusion" is the finding we obtained from the mathematical modeling. For example, the linear equation (1.1) in the above model is the "conclusion." The "model" in the above example is a generic linear equation ($Y = a + bX$) the economist uses to describe the data. The 8 year data for money supply increase rate and GDP growth rate in the above example is the "data" in the equation (1.2). The "logic" refers to the mathematical method used to obtain parameters for the "model." For example, an economist may use a statistical method to reduce the standard deviation when determining the parameters a or b in the generic linear equation. This statistical method is the "logic." The left side is equal to the right side. They are the same. Before we obtain the "conclusion", it is already embedded in the model, data, and the logic.

$$\text{conclusion} = \text{logic (assumptions, variables)} \qquad (1.3)$$

In theoretical economic research, the "conclusion" is determined by "assumptions," "variables," and the "logic." For instance, "most people at market are motivated by self-interest" is an assumption. "Interest rate", and "profit rate" are examples of "variables". The word "logic" in (1.3) refers to such logical process such as deduction and inference. Before we reach our conclusion, our assumptions, variables, and logic already determine what we can obtain.

The conclusion from theoretical research is economic theory. The conclusion obtained from the empirical economic research is economic modeling. Economic modeling is often not universally applicable. It is restricted by time, geography, nation, culture, etc. For instance, one may find that in the U.S. the consumer saving rate goes up as the interest rate increases, while one may also find during the same period of time, in China the consumer saving rate goes down as the interest rate increases. In the above example, the data only covers the years 1990 to 1997. Therefore, the model may be best used to predict for the years 1990 -1997. Applying the linear relations (Equation 1.1) to any year beyond 1997 is risky business, since we have no way to guarantee the accuracy of the prediction. Economic theory, however, can be applied universally without the limitations on time or nation.

There is nothing wrong with doing empirical research by applying mathematical modeling of economy. What is not appropriate is some economists were misled to believe mathematical modeling is the way to do theoretical economic research. As a result of this misunderstanding, progress in theoretical economics has been at a minimum for the past 100 years.

DEFINITION OF THE SUBJECT

It is important for readers to understand the subject matters studied in this book. The subject of this study is the market economy. This is not a study of a centralized, planned economy. A market economy can exist in a capitalist society, such as Japan, or in a socialist society, such as China. The theory presented here is developed through an analysis of the market economy in its abstract sense. What is an abstract of the market economy? What do the market economies of Japan, Germany, China, and the United States have in common? The common element in all market economies is the market: the place where people produce, and sell goods and services, not for self-consumption, but rather for the market. Therefore, this theory may be applied to any market economy regardless of its ideology or time. Typically mathematical modeling of economy is based on time series data; any attempt to make predictions beyond this range involves risk. For example, if a model is based on data from 1940-2000, we will not have much confidence to use this model to predict what will happen in the year 2040. However, the application of economic theory will not be limited by time like mathematical modeling.

A traditional market is a place where the buyers of goods and services meet sellers of goods and services. For example, some villagers and farmers in China meet every two weeks at a selected location to exchange goods and services. Farmers often walk several hours to get to the market in order to sell or purchase goods. In a developed metropolitan areas, the market is where the shops are, or where the shopping mall is located. There are also non-traditional markets where buyers and sellers do not meet. For example, the telephone book is a market where buyers can locate sellers. Without having to meet in person, goods and services can often be purchased with a telephone call. For example, Internet commerce makes it possible to make all kinds of transactions through a computer. Books, CDs, computers, and many other goods and services can be purchased on line. If we examine market changes along a time line, we will discover the following trends: 1. The market grows bigger geographically over time. When farmers in China meet, most people travel no more than 20 kilometers. This distance determines what commodities are available at the local market. With the introduction of the automobile, the train, the airplane, the telephone and the Internet, the market size grows from local to regional to global. 2. As the market develops, the time restriction gradually disappears. When the farmers in China meet every two weeks, goods and services can obviously be purchased every two weeks. The introduction of previously described modern convenience means that the market becomes available day and night, possibly even 24 hours a day, 7 days a week. Today one can purchase a book, toy, or other goods or services from the comfort of home without any time restrictions as long as you have a computer, Internet connection, and a major credit card. The selling process has become computerized and automatic. 3. As the market develops, the volume of goods and services available through a market increases, as does the total volume of transactions.

Economics is the study of the most efficient means of resource allocation. The objective of economic study is to improve economic conditions with respect to economic efficiency, via an understanding of how the economic system works. With higher economic efficiency, a market economy can develop faster. It can achieve a higher growth rate with less waste, as economic resources are more efficiently utilized. The objective of economic theory is to discover the inner mechanisms of the market economy. To understand the definition of the economics, we will discuss the terms used in the definition, specifically the terms "resources" and "efficiency".

What are economic resources? For mainstream economists, almost everything that requires a human decision as to how, when, and how much to use it, is an economic resource. Some examples are land, air, oil, minerals, and water to name a few.

To see how resource allocation is related to economic efficiency, let us examine two real world situations: Scenario 1, if you have a given amount of money, and you are given the choice of purchasing either a motorcycle or a car, which one would you pick? Is using a car instead of a motorcycle a more efficient way to allocate your limited resources? In the U.S. today, more people drive cars than motorcycles. However, a motorcycle is about 10 times less expensive and consumes only a fraction of the fuel needed to drive a car for the same distance. What is the correct decision?

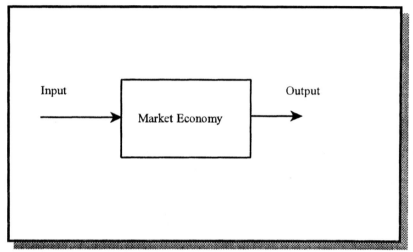

Figure 1.2   Input and Output

If you are a manufacturer, and you are given a choice between using electricity or fossil fuel, which would you choose? What if your choice also maximizes the efficiency of the whole economy? Perhaps you do not really care if the choice you make benefits society as a whole. In the market economy today, a manufacturer will compare the cost of the two sources of energy and select the one that is less expensive in order to maximize profit. Does the manufacturer's decision, based on profit maximization, also result in maximizing the efficiency of the economy?

Exactly what is economic efficiency? Generally speaking, the term "efficiency" refers to the input and output relationship of a system. For a given input, the higher the output, the higher the efficiency of the system. In economics, the system refers to the market economy where goods and services are produced, distributed, exchanged, and allocated by the market mechanism---the "invisible hand" as Adam Smith calls it. In this book, the term economic efficiency refers to the desired output related to the input of labor. Imagine a market economy as a box with inputs and outputs, referring to Figure 1.2. The input is human labor, and the output is the desired products or service. For a given set of desired outputs, the less labor we use to produce, the more efficient the system. In other words, efficiency of the economy is higher if the desired output, which takes into account the cost for controlling undesired byproducts, is higher for a given input of labor. What exactly is the desired output with consideration of the undesired byproducts? Consider the following example of a chemical manufacturer who produces a synthetic fiber that can be used for clothing. Assume 1 ton of toxic chemical waste for every 5 tons of desired synthetic fiber. Also assume that it takes 500 labor hours to produce the synthetic fiber, and 100 labor hours to convert the toxic chemical waste to a material that is socially acceptable and permitted by law. (All indirect labor inputs, such as machinery, energy, and raw material are converted to labor hours for simplicity of discussion.) From the whole economic system point of view (refer to Figure 1.2), the 5 tons of desired synthetic fibers cost not only the 500 labor hours required for production, but also the additional 100 labor hours required to eliminate the undesired byproducts. Therefore, the 5 tons of synthetic fiber will cost the economy as a whole a total of 600 labor hours to produce.

Why doesn't the economic efficiency account for the use of natural resources, machinery, energy, and other production input? In mainstream economics, "economics" is defined as the study of scarce resource allocation, and the term "resources" refers to all inputs in a production and manufacturing process. Literally this can mean anything, including raw materials, natural resources, capital, technology, equipment, and even time. In this book, which presents the study of economics from a different perspective, the term is defined differently. In this book, the term "economic resources," in the context of economic efficiency, refers only to human labor. The rationale behind this definition is as follows. The sole purpose of economic activity is to produce goods and services for human consumption, and the goal of human economic activity within the system is to produce more and more goods and services for a given amount of labor. The goal for the economist is to tune the market economy so that it maximizes the amount of goods and services produced for each labor hour. Furthermore, it is the productivity of labor that we care about. When we compare the wealth of nations, we compare not only the total GDP (Gross Domestic Product), but also the per capita real GDP. The nation that has the highest per capital real GDP is the "richest" nation , and the nation in which people enjoy the highest standard of living. In the real world, business people seek profit maximization, employees seek to maximize salary and income for a given labor hour input, and engineers seek to maximize performance with given materials. So, we have our first conclusion: people want to maximize the goods and services they can get from their given input in the economic system. Therefore, the best economic system is the one that can produce the highest output of goods and services with one average labor hour. Thus, labor hour input into the system (Figure 1.2) is the only input, and the only economic resource.

Imagine this: an economy is just a system we study. We use a box (Figure 1.2) to represent the economy. There is an input to the box and there are outputs from the box. The input is human labor, and the outputs are the goods and services consumed by people. What we care about is how much output the economy can produce for the average human labor per unit of time. From the economic efficiency point of view, labor input is the only resource we will investigate, since labor input is also the only input we use against output in order to measure economic efficiency. Consider the following points: we do not maximize the output per machine, we do not even maximize the output of crops per acre of land, since neither the machine nor the land demands a return. Only human beings demand a return on their work, investment, or technology. The sole purpose of human economic activity is to serve the human demand for goods and services, not a machines demand, not the land's demand. This is why I will exclude other resources when economic efficiency is investigated. When I use the terms "output" or "goods or services," I refer to the goods and services that are actually realized – those that are demanded by society and are actually paid for. If 10 million pairs of shoes are stored in a warehouse and cannot be sold at a market, these 10 million pairs of shoes are not realized. They are not to be counted in the output, nor are they considered part of the goods and services produced by the economy. Unsalable goods and services are a waste.

There are many real world examples to illustrate that people demand less input and more output. For example, an employee asks their manager for a raise in salary. The employee is asking to have more output for his given input. In financial markets, investors want more return on their investments, regardless of whether it is stock or bonds. The investors want more output for a given input. Have you ever heard a raw material asks for more return for its given input? Have you ever heard a machine (a form of capital) demand return for its given input? Of course not! For these reasons, I will consider human labor input as the only resource for the economic analysis below. Thus, economic efficiency of an economy can be presented by the following equation:

economic efficiency = total desired economic output / total labor input

The desired economic output refers to the products and services desired for human consumption. For example, when clean air becomes our desired product, we push the government to produce laws prohibiting pollution. Manufacturers spend more money and labor to reduce or eliminate pollution. As a result, we have clean air, which is a product -- the desired living environment. The total labor input refers to all the labor used in producing the goods and services a society needs. It only counts for the realized labor. When a shoemaker produces shoes that have been sold at markets, the shoemaker's labor is considered realized. If the shoemaker spends 100 hours making 100 pairs of shoes, and he cannot sell any of them at the market, the 100 hours used to make the 100 pairs of shoes are not realized labor. To be realized labor, the products or services produced by the labor hour must be sold at markets.

If we only consider labor as input, how do we deal with capital and raw materials? In the modern market economy, capital, labor, and raw materials are the major inputs of production. Capital is used to purchase machinery and labor that are used to produce a product that a business can sell at the market. Raw materials are necessary for certain industries such as the steel and chemical industries. However, capital and raw materials are not explicitly accounted in the above equation, even though they are important elements of production. Under this theory, capital and raw materials are considered simply different forms of labor. Since the purpose of human economic activity is to satisfy human desires and needs for goods and services with minimum labor input, it is only logical to think of capital, raw materials, and other forms of production input in terms of the amount of human labor spent to make, convert, and acquire. Thus, capital is accumulated past labor. Raw materials, when delivered to the starting point of production, also contain accumulated past labor.

In mainstream economics, the definition of economics stresses that the resources being studied are scarce. However, economic reality does not confirm such a judgement. The economic reality of today is that almost no market economy can reach the 100% employment rate. Most economies experience some unemployment, often ranging from 2% to more than 10%. There are many unemployed people all over the world looking for work. Scarce resources refer to resources that are insufficient to meet a demand, so if there are unemployed people, there is labor to spare. Thus, human labor cannot be considered a scarce resource. Although labor shortages do occasionally occur, they are not a persistent problem in any economy. Labor in most times is, if anything, in a state of surplus.

THE VALUE OF GOODS AND SERVICES

In this section, I will discuss how the value of goods comes into the question of economic resource allocation.

Goods and services are produced by an economy in order to satisfy the needs and wants of consumers. Suppose Kathy makes $30,000 net income after tax, and she will spend the money on housing, transportation, food, medical care, entertainment, recreation, etc. How can she decide how much she will spend on each type of consumption? Kathy will not be able to decide the consumption pattern unless she knows the relative cost of these items. By obtaining the information on the relative cost of these items, can she decide how much of her income she will spend on each type of goods and service. The money she has to spend, in this case, $30,000, limits the amount of goods and services she can consume. There are three factors that determine how a consumer will spend money: the consumer's personal preference, the consumer's purchasing power (money), and the price of the goods.

Among the three factors, the price of goods is directly related to the efficiency of resource allocation, while the personal preference and purchasing power are not directly related to the efficiency of the resource allocation. Let's first examine personal preference while holding the other two factors (prices and purchasing power) constant. Imagine that there are two consumers: John and Allen. John purchases a blue hat, and Allen purchases a green hat. The difference between the decision of the two consumers is the result of their personal preference. This does not result in any change of economic efficiency, because the objective of the economy is to satisfy the wants and needs of consumers. Consider a different case. John and Allen both purchase a means of transportation. John decides it is best for him to take the train to get to work in downtown New York, while Allen decides to drive a motorcycle. John wants to relax on the train to and from work. Allen would like to save time, even though it costs a little more money than taking the train. Since the purpose of economic activity is to produce goods and services to satisfy the needs and wants of consumers, no matter how consumers decide on what to consume, the efficiency of the economy is not affected. Similarly, purchasing power is not directly linked to the efficiency of the economy either. What consumers have to spend is not related to the efficiency with which goods and services are produced. The price of goods is directly linked to the efficiency of the economy. As I explained above, the essential input of any economic system is human labor. The human labor input is the sole resource we consider for economic resource allocation. To maximize economic efficiency, economic decisions should be made in such a way that the output for a given input (human labor) is maximized. For instance, suppose a pair of genuine leather shoes contains more human labor than that of a pair of shoes made with synthetic materials. The consumer has no preference for the material. They both create the same level of satisfaction for the consumer and meet the consumer's needs. What if the shoes made from the genuine leather are cheaper than the pair of shoes with synthetic materials, assuming other unmentioned parameters held constant? Suppose the pair of leather shoes is marked as $26.00 a pair, and nearby, shoes of synthetic material are priced as $84.00 a pair. Since both pairs of shoes meet the consumer's needs and create the same level of satisfaction, the consumer would certainly want to save money by purchasing the less expensive leather shoes. This sounds reasonable, but it creates a problem for the economy. Since a pricing structure of this nature leads the consumers to purchase more of the goods that consume more human labor to produce, while both goods produce the same level of satisfaction, as a result economic efficiency is reduced. As these examples show, the essence of all economic questions comes down to price determination. Because price determination is so important, the two central questions of this book are: How is the price determined? Furthermore, how should it be determined?

In industrial decision making, the price also plays a critical role. Never would a corporation pay its contractors whatever high price they desire for the goods and services they provide. The two most important factors in considering where to obtain business goods and services are price and quality. When quality is the same for two goods or services, price determines the allocation of the essential economic resource - human labor. In the business decision making process, when price does not correctly reflect the amount of human labor (economic resource) used to produce it, economic efficiency may decrease. For example, suppose Corporation Z needs to ship its product from New York to Los Angeles. There are two ways to ship: by truck, or by train. While everything else is equal, the truck shipping method actually uses more human labor than that of the train. (The human labor includes indirect human labor input--the amounts that are converted from capital, fuel, and other forms of input.) Suppose the train company charges $300 for the shipment, while the truck company charges them $200 for the shipment. Since Corporation Z wants to make more profit, it will ship its product by truck. In doing so, Corporation Z will have saved $100.00 for each shipment. However, from the economic efficiency point of view, the decision Corporation Z made reduces the economic efficiency, since truck shipment actually uses more human labor than that of train shipment.

Thus, the study of economic efficiency must lead to the study of price movement and determination. Understanding how prices are determined and how they should be determined is the key in deciphering the market economic system.

Price is the most elusive subject for economic study. As we know in a market economy, anyone can offer any price, even for the same goods and services. If John bought a television from a local shopping mall, John can try to resell it at ten times the price he paid for it. The only problem is that John will have a hard time convincing anybody to pay that price for the television. Since the offering price can be any random number, we can only base our study on the realized price, at which transactions actually happen. But even the study of realized price is much too difficult. We know the price of goods in the market economy changes with supply and demand for the goods and services. As demand increases, prices will usually increase also, assuming everything else holds equal. On the other hand, when demand deceases, prices also decrease. The price is also called the exchange value. Therefore, if we follow the movement of prices as they travel up and down, we will have little chance of catching anything meaningful. We need to introduce a new concept: the average exchange value. This is the average of the realized prices of goods or services. For example, consider Table 1.3 showing gasoline prices in Hong Kong during a given period of time. (All data are hypothetical):

Table 1. 3

Price	$1.23	$1.24	$1.25
Quantity Gallon	2300	1600	800

The average price of gasoline for the day is equal to

$$(1.23 \times 2300 + 1.24 \times 1600 + 1.25 \times 800)/(2300 + 1600 + 800)$$
$$= \$1.236809$$

So the average price of gasoline on that particular day is about $1.236809. In other words, the average exchange value of the gasoline when expressed in U.S. dollars is $1.236809.

SUMMARY

Economic efficiency has to do with one essential economic resource – human labor. Both consumer and business economic decision making rely on prices. A change in price can change the allocation of economic resources. Thus, price is the pivotal point in economic resource allocation. Since price plays such an important role in economic resource allocation, it must be the major subject of economic study. However, since the study of general price is difficult, we, therefore, study only the realized price. Since the realized prices of goods and services are subject to market demand and supply, we create a concept called average exchange value, which is the average realized price.

THE PAST LABOR THEORY OF VALUE

There are many past economists who have studied and made significant contributions to the labor theory of value. The two major economists who studied exchange value and have the most significant influence are Karl Marx and Adam Smith.

Karl Marx and Adam Smith developed the labor theory of value. The following presentation of labor theory of value by Adam Smith and Karl Marx is intended to acknowledge the contribution that past economists have made and to present it as a developmental step of the new labor theory of value. The concepts of these past theories can also serve as a good introduction to my labor theory of value.

THE LABOR THEORY OF ADAM SMITH

Adam Smith (1723-1790) was a Scottish economist. In March 1776, he published "An Inquiry into the Nature and Causes of the Wealth of Nations," which developed several different ways to explain price, the exchange value of goods. He seems not to be bothered by the conflicting explanation of how exchange values of goods are determined. Here I will only introduce his labor theory of value and his thoughts on the market mechanism, which Smith called the "invisible hand."

Smith argued that to increase the wealth of a nation, the government should rely on the self interest of people. He wrote: " It is not from the benevolence of the butcher, the brewer, or the baker, that we expect our dinner, but from their regard to their own interest."[1] Self interest is the motivation that drives the market mechanism to function. It is one of the conditions necessary for the market economy to function.

In his analysis of the early state of the economy (before capital and land become major factors in price determination), Smith found: "If among a nation of hunters, for example, it usually costs twice the labour to kill a beaver which it does to kill a deer, one beaver should naturally exchange for or be worth two deer. It is natural that what is usually the produce of two days' or two hours' labour, should be worth double of what is usually the produce of one day's or one hour's labour."[2] Smith also discovered that if it takes more hardship to produce beaver by one labor hour; beaver will be worth more at the market than the other product of one labor hour, which requires less hardship to produce. The exchange value of goods is also related to the skill, talent, and training needed to produce the goods. The higher the skill, talent, and training required, the higher the worth of

---

[1]Adam Smith, Wealth of Nation, Book 1, Chapter 2.
[2]Adam Smith, Wealth of Nation, Book1, Chapter 6.

goods produced by one hour labor.

Adam Smith observed that the word "value" has two meanings. One is use value, which refers to the usefulness of goods. The other is exchange value, which refers to the ability of the commodity to exchange other goods at the market. The commodity that has great use value often has no value in exchange. For example, air is very useful for humans to survive; no one can live without air. However, under common circumstances, air has no exchange value. In other words, no one will pay for air, since it is free. Conversely, a diamond may have very limited use, but it can have great exchange value.

One of the major contributions of Adam Smith is the concept of the division of labor. He proclaimed that division of labor is a major reason for productivity improvement. The division of labor is limited by the size of the market. Furthermore, the development of the market is a result of the division of labor.

According to Adam Smith, the exchange value of a commodity to the owner is the same as the amount of labor the commodity enables him to purchase and also the same amount of labor needed for him to acquire and exchange for it. Thus, labor is the real determinant of the exchange value for all commodities, but the real measure of exchange value by labor hours used in producing a commodity is not sufficient. Consideration must also be given to hardship, ingenuity, skill, and knowledge used in the production of such a commodity. Two hours of easy work may equal one hour of hard labor. Frequently, people exchange goods for goods without referring to the labor embedded within the goods, for exchange value is an abstract concept. Adam Smith concluded that labor alone is the ultimate and real standard for measuring the exchange value of commodities at all times and all places. Money is only a nominal price.

Smith also proclaimed that as individuals pursue their own interests and gains for their own security and benefit, the "invisible hand" will direct his or her effort to promote the public goods and to produce the greatest value for society often more effectively than he intends to promote, even though he did not know, nor intend, to promote the greatest benefit to society. The "invisible hand" is the market mechanism. It directs production, distribution and consumption by means of price fluctuation. It tells us what to produce, and how much to produce. It also tells consumers what to save and what to consume. Also the "invisible hand" provides material incentive to individuals to respond to market price changes. Adam Smith seems to believe that the "invisible hand" is a perfect mechanism to bring the greatest value and public benefit to society.

He was partially right about the market economic system. However, as I shall present in the following chapters, the market is not a perfect system. It often does not operate at peak economic efficiency without human intervention. In other words, a free market system itself often cannot achieve an optimal economic operating condition.

THE LABOR THEORY OF VALUE BY KARL MARX

Karl Marx (1818-1883) was a German philosopher and economist. His major work is *Das Kapital* (1867-1894).

Marx started his analysis with use value and exchange value. He declared that use value is independent of exchange value, although a commodity must have a use value if it has an exchange value. He also explained the role of money.

Marx defines the term "socially necessary labor" as the average time needed to produce an article with average labor skill level and intensity in normal and typical circumstances of production. Socially necessary labor determines the value of commodities. The value of a commodity is measured by the socially necessary labor time to produce it.

As with Adam Smith's theory, I will only present the portion of his labor theory that serves as an introduction to my labor theory of value. Some of Karl Marx's ideas presented below are not correct according to my analysis. They are presented here for comparison with my theory, even though I disagree with certain of his points.

Marx's key discovery is the theory of surplus value. He argued that the labor hired by capitalists not only produces value that is sufficient to cover the wages paid to the human laborers, but also creates surplus value. During the production process, labor transfers the value of capital stocks to the final products. Capital stock can be machinery, equipment, or other forms of capital needed for a business. Surplus value is therefore the value that labor produces beyond the value paid by capitalists in the form of wages. Surplus value is profit to the capitalists. The term "Labor power" as used by Marx refers to the capacity of labor to produce use value. Labor power is a commodity in a capitalist society. The value of the labor power is determined by the socially necessary labor to provide the labor with food, training, shelter, etc. Suppose it takes an average of 6 hours of work per day to produce the goods necessary to sustain the laborer with consideration of its life long needs. Capitalists hire the labor power to work 8 hours a day, and only pay the laborer 6 hours of monetary compensation. The 2 hour difference is the surplus value. The surplus value is unearned income for capitalists. The 6 hours is the variable capital (v), and the 2 hours is surplus value (s). The exploitation rate is s/v. Marx has made several errors in the analysis of surplus value. The reason Marx is opposed to the ownership of private property is because he believes the private property generates unlabored income, which economists call "economic rent." Marx considers profit a form of surplus value. In addition to profit, on his list of things that generate surplus value, he includes interest and rents of land owned by the bourgeois class. Marx believes that surplus value has made the poor poorer, and the rich richer. His solution is to simply eliminate ownership of private property in order to get rid of the surplus value.

Marx believes society develops in stages. When capitalistic society develops to a certain level, a new form of society will replace capitalistic society. At that time, the social system of private property will be eradicated.

Marx's surplus value theory is not without problems. I will demonstrate in the following discussion that profit and interest are not necessarily surplus value as Marx has reasoned. When they are surplus value, they are often transitory. Today, land taxes (property taxes) have been implemented in many market economies, these land taxes (property taxes) greatly reduce the economic rent on land such that the surplus value produced by land has also been reduced. Although rent on land is surplus value, the surplus value in many economies has been taxed and reduced to a smaller percentage of the original value.

Just as the government can implement tax systems to reduce surplus value on economic rent of land, it is perhaps also possible to design a tax system that can reduce or even eliminate surplus values of all forms in an economic system as a whole. Marx suggests eliminating the private property system as a way to eliminate the surplus value. In an indirect way, he was actually suggesting to get rid of the market economy altogether. Without private property, the market economy would not be able to function, just as the "invisible hand" in the market economy cannot function without individuals promoting their self interest. The market economy requires a private property system to ensure that the individual who obtains goods and services from the market has both the rights to keep and accumulate wealth within the limit of law.

My recommendation for the surplus value problem is to use a tax system and government economic policy to reduce surplus value. As long as there is profit, interest and rent, the individual will pursue them without knowing they are also promoting the public good. If surplus value can be correctly dealt with, the market mechanism will be preserved, and private property will remain. The market can still function as an efficient resource allocation mechanism. As we know, centrally planned economies without a private property system do not work well. For example, the Soviet Union and China have experimented with a centralized and planned economy, and history shows that it does not work, because it does not provide a material incentive to production, for efficient resource allocation. Marx's surplus value theory is at best only partially correct.

The theoretical difference between Marx's labor theory of value and mine is that Marx developed the surplus value concept and deemed profit and interest undesirable. According to him, profit and interest are necessary exploitation of labor. It is therefore a transfer of value from labor to the capitalists without proper compensation to the laborer. According to the theory presented in this book, profit and interest are necessary for economic efficiency under normal circumstances. They are not exploitations of labor when the average rate of profit and the average rate of interest is within a certain range. Furthermore, the general theory of economic efficiency concludes that profit and interest are not all exploitation. In other words, they are not all unearned income.

THE CHALLENGE AGAINST THE LABOR THEORY OF VALUE

Many schools of economic thought have repeatedly attacked the classic labor theory of value. Some economists attack it because of an ideological bias. The following presents some well-known reasoning against the classic labor theory of value. My new ideas come from understanding and solving the following paradoxes. The resolution to the paradoxes presented in this section will be discussed in a later chapter, also.

PARADOX 1 (DIAMOND)

Several centuries ago, after one day of hard work in the corn field, a farmer walked back to his home. As he walked, he saw a shining stone in the field, and picked it up and examined it. It was a diamond. He took the stone to a market and sold it for 20 ounces of gold. This diamond which cost him no labor was equal to years of his farming. One year of hard labor in the corn field could only be exchanged for a fraction of the diamond's value. If the labor theory of value was correct, how can it be that a diamond took no labor to obtain has so much value, while the farmer's long hour of hard labor was worth so little?

PARADOX 2 (PAPER CURRENCY)

If Marx's labor theory of value is correct, that the value of goods is determined by the average labor hours it contains, why does paper money, which contains so few labor hours, have so much value?

PARADOX 3 (OLD WINE)

According to Marx's labor theory of value, the exchange value is determined by the labor necessary to produce the goods. If exchange value of goods is determined by the labor value, then how can old wine have a much higher exchange value than that of fresh wine? When wine is produced, the labor needed to produce it is fixed into the product. Simply keeping the wine for several decades should not increase the exchange value of the wine, according to Marx's labor theory of value. Yet, the reality is that old wine can sell for as much as 100 times the original price.

PARADOX 4 (WATER IN THE DESERT)

At a river side, a cup of water may be worth little or nothing at all. However, it is worth a lot of money for a thirsty traveler in the desert. Some economists claim that the exchange value is determined by marginal value. Water costs less near a river, because there is plenty of water. Therefore, the marginal utility of water is very low. In the desert, the water is scarce, so it will be worth more, since the marginal utility of the water increases as the total available water decreases. Therefore, the value of goods is not determined by the labor used to produce or reproduce them. It is instead determined by marginal utility.

PARADOX 5 (SCARCE COMMODITY)

Many rare commodities command inconceivably high prices at marketplaces, such as an old postal stamp, rare book, coin, artwork, or antique. The price that people are willing to pay for such a kind of scarce commodity is much higher than the labor needed to produce or reproduce the good. Thus, it is the marginal utility that determines the exchange value.

PARADOX 6 (LAND MARKET)

If the labor theory of value is correct, why is the price of land not zero? Land as we know it does not contain any labor; rather, it exists on earth through no human intervention. If it does not contain any labor value, it should cost nothing on the market, and no one should have to pay for a piece of land.

LOH'S THEORY OF VALUE

There are two values associated with goods. First, the goods can be used to exchange for other goods. This indicates that the goods must have some kind of value. This value is called exchange value. In addition to exchange for other goods, goods are useful. This is the use value.

THE NATURE OF USE VALUE

A house provides a place to live where people can be protected against cold winters, hot summers, storms, and winds. These are some of the use values for a house. Television brings news, entertainment, and educational programs to one's home. This is the use value of a television. Use value may change from time to time. One reason for such a change is technology and scientific development. Before the Chinese developed silk-making techniques, there was little use value for the silkworm. Science and technology turn many goods that have no use value into goods that have a good deal of use value.   Use value depends on human knowledge of the good. A diamond may not have had any use value 2000 years ago, before humans discovered cosmetic uses for diamonds.

Use value can also be divided into two categories: one is use value for consumers; the other is use value for businesses. Use value can also be enhanced or diminished by advertisement or cultural changes.

Furthermore, use value can be divided into potential use value and realized use value. An airplane can transport people to work on a daily basis. This is the potential use value of an airplane. However, most people probably get to work every day by automobile or bus, rather than flying an airplane, simply because the airplane is too costly. So, the airplane has a potential use value as a commuting vehicle, but has no realized use value as a commuting vehicle.

The realized use value is also related to the exchange value. Gold is not used to build a public bathroom. This is not because it cannot be used to build bathrooms. It is because gold is too expensive to be used in public bathrooms. It is simply not economical. Perhaps only the very wealthy and royalty have the luxury to use gold in bathrooms. The realized use value may increase as its exchange value decreases. However, for some goods, people purchase them for their high prices, since these people believe the high price tag gives them a greater status. A decrease in the price may actually decrease the use value, such as a very expensive luxury automobile or a piece of jewelry. For consumer goods, use value satisfies the consumers' physical, biological, or psychological needs. Goods must have use value before they can have exchange value. However, goods that have use value may not have exchange value. For example, air has use value. It is important to human survival, but in normal circumstances there is no exchange value for air.

There are goods on the market, and there are bads on the market too. Goods are merchandise produced to satisfy the wants and needs of consumers or businesses. Goods are what people want. Bads are usually undesired byproducts of production processes, and things people want to get rid of. For example, in a well regulated economy, consumers are not allowed to dump their trash anywhere they like, because they will receive fines. Instead, people pay a service charge to hire a business to get rid of their trash. The trash does not have any positive use value. It has a negative use value. It does not have positive exchange value either. It has negative exchange value. Polluted air, water, and sewage are examples of bads. Items that have zero use value will also have zero exchange value.

THE NATURE OF EXCHANGE VALUE

The exchange value of goods fluctuates around an invisible value. This value is the average exchange value, and it is also called the labor value necessary to produce the goods.

Several hundred years ago, economists asked how two goods were exchanged at marketplaces. For example, why were two sheep exchanged for a horse at a marketplace? To use modern examples, we will ask why an automobile costs $20,000, as well as why a bicycle is cheaper than an automobile. In essence, economists were trying to understand why a particular quantity of good A is exchanged for a particular quantity of good B. This book provides answers for many of the paradoxes and contradictions, which the previous economic theory of value could not resolve.

Many economic theories were developed in the past in attempts to explain what determines value of goods. The theory of labor value is only one of many attempts. The marginal theory of value, created by economists to replace Marx's labor theory of value, will be explained in a later chapter as to why marginal theory of value is logically false. However, the consumer utility theory created by marginal economists is a very useful tool. This book will present how consumer utility theory is combined with labor theory of value to create an ideal economy. In the analysis process of an ideal economy, optimal economic parameters are obtained. Thus the consumer utility theory, used by marginal economists, combined with the labor theory of value, fit together to become a unified economic theory.

The values of goods are measured by their ability to exchange for other goods. Consider the following hypothetical example. One kilogram of gold has more exchange value than one kilogram of cotton. (All examples in the following discussion are hypothetical. A real case example would be accompanied by citation.) For example, a kilogram of gold is exchangeable for 120 pairs of shoes, while a kilogram of cotton can only be exchanged for 1 pair of shoes. In the above example, the 1 kilogram of cotton has an exchange value of one pair of shoes, while the 1 kilogram of gold has an exchange value of 120 pairs of shoes. One kilogram of gold has thus 120 times the exchange value of 1 kilogram of cotton. The value of a good is measured by its exchange value against other goods.

The measurement of the value of goods by money changes over time. In the history of economies, gold, silver, and other objects were once used as money. When gold was used as money, people measured the value of merchandise by gold, instead of shoes as discussed in a previous example. If we were to use gold to measure the exchange value of goods today, we would perhaps say that the value of a car is worth about 50 ounces of gold, and a color TV is worth about 2 ounces of gold. Money, such as gold, is just one kind of good, that has certain characteristics which make it suitable to be the medium of commodity exchange. Materials that are light in weight, high in exchange value, dividable, nonperishable, stable in value, and easy to carry are most likely to become money. Today, most countries no longer use gold as the currency standard. Paper currency is prevalent today. In the future, we may see digital currency.

In the modern market economy, we measure the value of goods by how much money we pay for them, and how much money they are worth if we were to sell the goods. In short, we use paper money to measure the value of goods.

How does one find regularity in price movement? In everyday life, we see changes in the prices of goods sold. Prices of goods sometimes go up and other times go down. These price changes do not seem to follow any rules. However, the prices move up and down over time around the labor value of the goods. Think of the ocean. In the ocean, if we observe 1 square foot area of ocean, we would hardly discover any pattern of movement. It seems that the ocean waves move in an irregular fashion. Wave after wave of water comes and goes. If we observe a larger area over a longer period of time, we would be able to discover the average water level changes over time during a day, a month, and even a year. The fluctuation in exchange value of goods is very similar to that of ocean waves. If we take a broader view and a longer period of observation, we can find the underlying pattern of movement.

MARKET MODEL 1 (WITHOUT CAPITAL)

The new theory of value is introduced in this book in two different ways. In the first chapter, the theory of value is introduced by investigating how the real market system works. In the second chapter, the theory of value is introduced again by asking how it should work in an ideal economy.

The following section introduces the core of the new labor theory of value by analyzing a number of market models in an attempt to answer how the market works. I will start with a very simple model -- Market Model 1, then move on to a more complex model. In doing so, we are trying to answer these questions: How does the market work? What are the rules of market exchange? What are the assumptions of this simple market model? What conclusions could we get from this simple market model?

Table 1. 4   Market Model 1 (without capital)

	Beef (Wang)	Pork (Zhang)
Labor hours needed to produce one kg of meat	4 hours	2 hours

Suppose we have two families: The Wang family and the Zhang family. Each family is a production unit. (All numbers used here are hypothetical.) There are two goods: beef and pork. Suppose the two families change goods via a barter market, and production does not require capital. Both families enjoy the same level of productivity. It will take an average of 4 hours to produce a kilogram (kg) of beef regardless of which family produces it. It will take 2 hours to produce a kilogram (kg) of pork regardless of which family produces it.

Assume the Wang family only produces beef, and the Zhang family only produces pork. To help remember this, I write (Wang) by the word "beef" and (Zhang) by the word "pork" (Table 1.4). When Mr. Wang and Mr. Zhang meet at a market, at what price will the exchange happen? Mr. Wang comes to the barter market and wants to get pork. Mr. Wang will ask for at least 2 kg of pork for his 1 Kg of beef, because he knows it takes about twice as long to produce the beef. That is, Mr. Wang knows it takes him 4 hours of work to produce 1kg of beef; he also knows that if he were to raise pigs it would take him about half the amount of time needed for each kilogram of beef, which is 2 hours of labor. He certainly does not want to be short-changed.

For similar reasons, Mr. Zhang will ask for at least 1 kg of beef

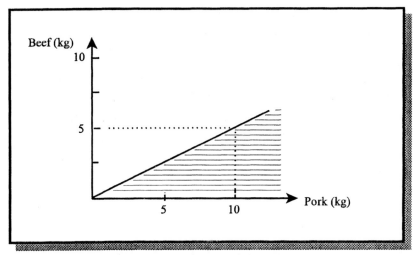

Figure 1.3   Acceptable Trade Area for Wang

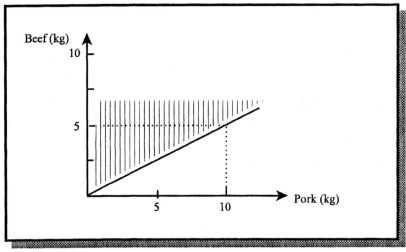

Figure 1.4   Acceptable Trade Area for Zhang

for his 2 kg of pork. Therefore, the final exchange will be 1 kg of beef for 2 kg of pork. The price of beef per kg is 2 kg of pork. Conversely, the price of pork per kg is 0.5 kg of beef. The shaded area in Figure 1.3 illustrates the acceptable trade area for Mr. Wang. The shaded area in

Figure 1.4 illustrates the acceptable trade area for Mr. Zhang.

Combining Figure 1.3 and Figure 1.4, and we can determine that the acceptable trade for both Mr. Wang and Mr. Zhang is the straight line shown in Figure 1.5.

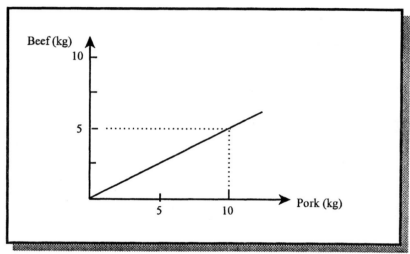

Figure 1.5   Acceptable Trade for Both Wang and Zhang

SUMMARY OF ASSUMPTIONS FOR MARKET MODEL 1

The above example is the simplest market model. The discussion above implies the following assumptions:

1.   Each participant can switch to and from one trade to the other, such as switching from producing beef to pork. There is no restriction in switching between the production of the different goods. The producer can decide what to produce, when, where, how, and what quality to produce. There is also free entry to production, and free flow of the factors of production and consumption. Each producer also has information on other producers.

2.   The market model shows the equilibrium point at which the exchange of goods happens. At equilibrium the goods are exchanged according to the value of labor used to produce them. When the quantity supplied is greater than the quantity demanded or vice versa, the exchange of goods does not happen at equilibrium.

3.   People at the market are motivated by their own material interest. They want to gain as much as possible in an exchange of goods at the market. Generally speaking, people are selfish.

4.   All the participants in the market have the same level of productivity for a good. They all have the same skills.

5.   Market Model 1 is a barter market; no money is involved.

6.   Production is comprised of labor only. It does not include capital and other material costs. It is static, and does not incorporate changes, such as improvement of productivity over time. It does not take time into consideration at all.

SUMMARY OF CONCLUSION FOR MARKET MODEL 1

At equilibrium, goods are exchanged according to the value of labor used to produce them under the above assumptions.

INTRODUCTION TO THE REST OF THE MODELS

These six assumptions make Market Model 1 extremely simple, and therefore, very far from reality. Obviously, a theory that stops here would not be terribly useful since it could not be applied to real market conditions. To remedy this, we will relax or change each assumption in turn, one at a time, and discuss the implications and findings that this has on our market model, until finally we reach a set of conditions that is as close to reality as is theoretically possible.

We will begin by discussing assumptions in the simple Market Model 1. Relaxing it will cause changes in market conditions, leading to a slightly different market model. As each assumption is considered, the market model will change. Each set of changes will be indicated as belonging to a market model of a different stage. Table 1.5 illustrates what we are going to discuss, which model is for which assumptions, what conditions are the focus of the discussion for that market model, and what

Table 1. 5   Market Model and Focus of Discussion

Model Number	Assumption Number	Focus of Discussion
2	2	How does the market react to changes in supply or demand?
3	3	How does the market react to altruism commodity exchange behavior?
4	4	How does the market work when producers' productivity differs?
5	5	Introduction of money into the market model.
6	6	Introduction of capital into the market with single commodity.
7	6	Introduction of capital into market, with currency and dual commodities.
8	6	Studies the average profit rate, inflation, and wage rate, with currency, dual commodities.
9	6	Separation of laborer and capital.
10	6	Separation of laborer and capital under full employment (deflation).
11	6	Separation of laborer and capital, full employment (without deflation).

we are trying to discover. As the market model conditions approach those of reality, some market stages must be considered under different conditions.

Table 1.5 Continued:

Model Number	Assumption Number	Focus of Discussion
12	6	Separation of laborer and capital, less than full employment, deflation.
13	6	Separation of laborer and capital, less than full employment, no deflation.

MARKET MODEL 2

In this model, we will be concerned with assumption 2 in Market Model 1. Assumption 2 states: "The market model shows the equilibrium point at which the exchange of goods happens. At equilibrium the goods are exchanged according to the value of labor used to produce them. When the quantity supplied is greater than the quantity demanded or vice versa, the exchange of goods does not happen at equilibrium."

The objective of Market Model 2 is to discover how a market works when the quantity supplied is greater than the quantity demanded or vice versa.

The price of goods shifts up and down as demand and supply change. Price movement is centered around the social average labor hour used to produce the goods. The word "social" refers to the way in which the average labor hour is determined: by all the producers of the product in a society, not just one particular producer. The social average labor hour is also called the labor value. The price fluctuation of goods is centered around the labor value of the goods. Price may fluctuate above or below labor value. Labor value is realized only when the product is exchanged at the market.

This model will demonstrate that there is a natural force to move the price toward the labor value. To illustrate, consider the following market model. Suppose Mr. Wang and Mr. Zhang are now two producers at a bigger market. This means that there are other producers and buyers, and Mr. Wang and Mr. Zhang thus cannot control the market price. Use the above Market Model 1 in this new circumstance, where at equilibrium the price of 1 kg beef is 2 kg of pork.

Table 1. 6

	Beef (Wang)	Pork (Zhang)
Labor hours needed to produce one kg of meat	4 hours	2 hours

(Assume Mr. Zhang and Mr. Wang have the same level of productivity. They use the same amount of time to produce one kilogram of pork. They also use the same amount of time to produce one kilogram of beef.)

Table 1. 7   What product will Mr. Zhang produce?

	What to produce	Traded for
Option 1	Pork 6 kg	2 kg beef
Option 2	Beef 3 kg	9 kg pork

If the market price for 1 kg of beef rises to 3 kg of pork (from 2 kg of pork) due to a sudden increase in the demand for beef, Mr. Zhang will now find it more profitable to produce beef instead of pork. Suppose each producer has only 12 labor hours as input to the production. Given 12 labor hours, Mr. Zhang can produce 6 kg of pork. This can be traded for 2 kg of beef at the market. In other words, if Mr. Zhang produces only pork, he will have either 6 kg of pork, or 2 kg of beef. (If all pork is traded for beef.) If Mr. Zhang uses his 12 labor hours to produce beef, he will produce 3 kg of beef, which can be traded for 9 kg of pork. The options are summarized in Table 1.7. Therefore, for producers it is more profitable to produce beef than pork. As Mr. Zhang and other producers find it more profitable to produce beef, more producers will shift their production from pork to beef.

Assuming that the demand for beef has not changed as more beef is shipped to market, its price will fall. Eventually, the price of beef will fall toward the price level determined by the labor hours necessary to produce it, which is called the labor value of the beef.

At equilibrium, the price per kg of beef is 2 kg of pork. The price can also be represented directly by the labor hours it can command. In terms of labor hours, the price per kg of beef is 4 hours at equilibrium, because 2 kg of pork is equivalent to 4 labor hours. When the demand for beef increases, the price per kg of beef increases to 3 kg of pork. This price is equivalent to 6 labor hours, since 3 kg of pork is equivalent to 6 labor hours. When the demand for beef decreases, the price of beef falls below equilibrium level. Say the price per kg of beef becomes 1 kg of pork. That is equivalent to 2 labor hours, since it takes two labor hours to produce 1 kg of pork. What will happen to the market?

Table 1.8 illustrates when the beef price is below the equilibrium; Option 1 is much better off than Option 2. In this case, beef producers will find it more profitable to produce pork instead. More production capacity will be used to produce pork, while the beef production will be reduced. As beef production shrinks, the beef price will rise back until it reaches equilibrium.

Generally speaking, if the beef price is below the market equilibrium, market force (Smith's "invisible hand") will move the price up toward equilibrium. When the beef price is below the value of beef, which is the socially necessary labor to produce the beef, producers will find it more profitable to produce other products, such as pork, and beef production will be reduced. The price of beef will increase.

Table 1. 8   When beef price is below equilibrium

	What to produce	Traded for
Option 1	6 kg of pork	6 kg of beef
Option 2	3 kg of beef	3 kg of pork

CONCLUSION OF MARKET MODEL 2

In conclusion, the price will move toward the equilibrium where price equals the labor value needed to produce the goods. The changes in supply or demand of a good can cause the price of the good to move up or down. The market force will move the price toward equilibrium, which is equal to the labor value of the goods.

IMPLICATION OF MARKET MODEL 2

In this case, the equilibrium point is equal to the labor value of the goods. This happens only under perfect market conditions. However, the equilibrium point is not necessarily equal to the labor value of the good in all cases. If the market only functions partially, for example in land markets, the equilibrium price may not equal the labor value. This is because no one is able to take advantage of a higher price of land by producing more land and shipping it to the market, meanwhile making a nice profit and getting rich.

Under perfect market conditions, the market force automatically allocates resources for production and also directs the producers to produce more when quantity demanded by consumer increases, and less when the quantity demanded decreases. There is no need for a central planner to plan exactly what to produce, how many to produce, when to produce, where to produce, and what quality to produce.

MARKET MODEL 3

Next, we will discuss the third assumption in Market Model 1: "People at the market are motivated by their own material interest. They want to gain as much as possible in an exchange of goods at the market. Generally speaking, people are selfish." This assumption is the basis for the market economy.

However, in reality, there are people who are quite unselfish. What happens when there are altruistic people at the market? As we shall see below, if altruistic people participate in the market activity, they will be driven out of the market.

Consider a market where there are many buyers and sellers, including Mr. Wang and Mr. Zhang. Assume other things unchanged from Market Model 2. Let's consider a situation where Mr. Wang deliberately sells below the market price. As mentioned above in the previous Market Model 2, the market price for 1 kg beef is 2 kg of pork, which is the equilibrium price level. If Mr. Wang decides to sell his beef below the market price, there will always be other buyers who find this a good opportunity to make a profit. They will buy as much as Mr. Wang is willing to sell, and then they will resell the goods to the market again in order to make a profit.

Assume Mr. Wang is willing to sell 100 kg of beef for the price of 1 kg of pork, while the prevailing market price is 2 kg of pork for 1 kg of beef. Assume a trader by the name of Mr. Chen buys 100 kg of beef from Mr. Wang. He can then resell the beef at the market for the normal market price of 2 kg of pork. Mr. Chen spends 100 kg of pork for the 100 kg of beef from Mr. Wang. He then resells the 100 kg of beef at the market for 200 kg of pork. He just received 100 kg of pork simply by buying and selling anothers' product.

This can be viewed as Mr. Wang willingly transferring his labor hours to others, without asking for compensation. In a competitive market, Mr. Wang only produces a small fraction of the quantity of goods sold at the market; thus, his willingness to sell at a low price will not change how the market behaves. If Mr. Wang deliberately tries to sell above the market price, he will not be able to sell his product. Buyers have the selfish desire to purchase the same kind of goods of the same quality at the lowest price. As we can see from this example, the market will still function as it was before, even when some people are not selling and buying at the market equilibrium price.

If some altruistic people are willing to pay the above market price, the net result is that they transfer their labor hours to the sellers without being compensated. Conversely, if a buyer wants to buy below the market price, a buyer will have trouble finding a seller who will sell below the market price. Alternatively, we say that the altruistic person transfers his wealth to other people without compensation.

CONCLUSION OF MARKET MODEL 3

We conclude from the above analysis that the market force will still function even if some participants decide to buy or sell above or below the market price. The market only requires some people in the general population be selfish when participating in market exchanges in order for the market to function. When an altruistic person sells at below the market price or purchases above the market price, the person is actually transferring his labor hours to another person, without compensation.

MARKET MODEL 4 (PRODUCERS WITH DIFFERENT PRODUCTIVITY)

The assumption 4 of Market Model 1 states: " All the participants in the market have the same level of productivity for a good. They all have the same skills." Next, I will discuss assumption 4. Our objective is to answer this question: What happens if market participants do not have the same level of productivity when producing the same good? As the market develops, people will find it more profitable to concentrate on producing the good they are skilled at making. This market mechanism makes possible the division of labor. The division of labor refers to the specialization of labor used in production. Specialization means that people only work in the field or business in which they excel. They do not have to be a jack-of-all-trades. A typical consumer has many different needs, such as food, shelter, transportation, and an education. The consumer does not need to produce everything for him or herself; instead, the consumer will buy some goods at the market by exchanging goods or services with others. Without specialization of labor, the consumer would need to do all of the following in order to maintain a satisfactory standard of living: farm, raise livestock, fish, sew and make cloth, build a shelter, obtain clean water, make medicines and treat disease, etc. This list can go on and go. No one is able to do everything, and the level of productivity would be very low if one person had to do everything, anyway. Specialization allows a wider variety of goods to be available at market, since no one person can produce as many things as the whole economy. It also allows for increased productivity. Productivity is a measurement of average production output per labor hour. A wealthy nation will have a higher level of productivity than a poor nation. The scope of division of labor is limited only by the size of the market. The division of labor improves the productivity of labor in the following ways:

1.   Since specialization allows a worker to know more about the production process, the workers have a better chance of improving the production processes. If a worker needs to produce many different products and work with many different processes, it is unlikely that this worker will do well in any of his work. Specialization sharpens the workers' skills.

2.   Specialization makes it possible to have manufacturing--mass

production of a product. Mass production generates a natural need to use improved tools, equipment, and machinery for production. Those demands for advanced machinery also stimulate advancement in technology and science.

3.   Specialization requires special skills. Division of labor in production leads to the division of labor in engineering and science.

Suppose there are many producers at a market, as shown in Table 1.9. The currency we use here is hypothetical units of average social labor hours.

The numbers in Table 1.9 represent the cost of the products in average labor hours per kilogram. For example, it costs an average of 4 hours to produce 1 kg of beef for Mr. Wang. This table presents the difference in productivity. The lower the number, the higher is the productivity, and vice versa. The difference in productivity will lead to the division of labor.

Table 1. 9

Producer	Beef	Pork	Wheat
Wang	4	2	0.45
Zhang	3.5	2.2	0.5
Tang	4.1	1.9	0.47
Li	3.9	1.9	0.52

How will a central authority plan the production? How would an authority maximize the output for a given number of labor hours for each producer? Let's say each producer only has 1000 labor hours. The answer in this case is simple. Look at the product column to see who is the most productive producer for each product. Examine the column for beef, for instance. In this column, Mr. Zhang has the lowest cost. That is Mr. Zhang has the highest productivity among the four producers. For pork, Mr. Tang and Mr. Li are equally productive, because they have the lowest cost. Mr. Wang has the highest productivity for wheat. If we have Mr. Zhang produce beef, Mr. Wang produce wheat, and Mr. Tang and Mr. Li produce pork, we will have the production capacity optimized. The market as a whole will produce more products and wealth. In mathematical terms, this is a linear programming question.

How does the market automatically reach optimal resource allocation without a central authority's interventions as discussed above? Take the beef production, for example. As explained in the previous model, the producer wants to sell his product at or above his average labor hour used to produce the good. This will maximize his return, wealth or profit. For the beef, the acceptable price for each producer is listed below. (Price is in average labor hours)

Producer	Beef
Mr. Wang	≥4
Mr. Zhang	≥3.5
Tang	≥4.1
Li	≥3.9

If the market price for beef is at 4.0 labor hours, all producers will find it profitable to produce more beef, except Mr. Tang. He will get short-changed if he produces beef. The term profitable in the previous sentence refers to a situation in which the producer can sell goods at a price higher than the labor hours he put into producing them. For Mr. Tang, the market price of 4.0 labor hours is less than the labor hours he used to produce beef, so he does not profit by selling beef. It is better for him to produce other goods and obtain beef through exchange.

Mr. Zhang can sell beef that cost him 3.5 hours of labor for the price of 4.0 labor hours. The net gain is 0.5 labor hours (4.0 - 3.5 = 0.5) for every kg of beef he sells. Mr. Zhang, who is just as greedy as the average person, will want to have an even larger profit. First, he can reduce his production of other products and concentrate on beef. Second, he can hire people to work for him if his high productivity in beef production is the result of special skill or technique. This leads to a division of labor. As his beef production increases and more beef is sold at the market, the market price of beef will fall. As the price of beef falls, more and more producers will be driven out of beef production. For example, if the price drops to 3.95. Mr. Wang and Mr. Tang will be out of beef production, since Mr. Wang will need to sell the beef at a price of at least 4.0 labor hours to be worthwhile, and Mr. Tang will need to sell at least 4.1 labor hours per kg beef. As long as there are additional profits to be made, the producers will be motivated to produce more. This means that the price of goods will fall as close as possible to the number of labor hours used in producing the goods under perfect market conditions.

CONCLUSION OF MARKET MODEL 4

When one producer enjoys the highest level of productivity and the highest profits, other producers will try to imitate this producer. Others will gradually learn how to produce goods as productively as the best producer on the market. Price will be driven toward the labor value.

However, in imperfect markets, there is one superior producer, while other producers are prohibited from obtaining the skills or technology needed to reach the productivity of this superior producer. When this happens, the superior producer tries to maximize his profit by selling above the required labor hours. Thus, the superior producer monopolizes the market. The superior producer is a monopoly.

In a perfect market, price will move toward the lowest number of labor hours (or price) needed to produce the goods among multiple producers. Less efficient producers will be driven out of business.

When we apply this analysis of the market to all of the product listed above, we discover that the market optimally allocated each producer with the product that can give the producer the highest level of productivity. In this manner, the market selects the correct producer to produce the correct product.

Under perfect market conditions, the equilibrium point equals the labor value of the product. In other words, at an equilibrium point, exchange happens at equal exchange of value or exchange of equal value.

MARKET MODEL 5

The assumption 5 states: "Market Model 1 is a barter market; no money is involved." In Market Model 5, we will try to address these questions: What happens at market when money is introduced? What does money do? What is its function?

Today we rarely see a barter market. Most transactions are conducted by using currency. In each economy, a different currency is used. Money is a commodity, just like any other good. It provides a measure of value for other commodities. The average price of a commodity at an equilibrium in a competitive market reflects the value of the commodity. The value of the commodity is the socially necessary labor to produce and bring it to the market. Like the example given above, the value of beef was measured with pork in a barter market. Instead of pork, people in past centuries have used gold, silver, and many other objects as money. Eventually, government was unable to supply enough gold currency to meet the needs for economic development, and paper money was introduced. The introduction of money does not change the nature of the market. It only makes it easier for buyers and sellers to exchange goods. Money is the medium of exchange. In a barter market, a baker who wants a pair of shoes has to find a shoemaker, who at the same time also wants this baker's bread. If the shoemaker wants clothes instead of bread, no transaction can be made. Transactions in a barter market depend on the double coincidence of wants. Money makes it possible to have transactions without double coincidences.

Let's look at Market Model 1 again; this time we introduce money as the medium of exchange.

Suppose two producers exchange goods via a market, and production does not require capital. Both producers enjoy the same level of productivity. It will take an average of 4 hours to produce one kg of beef, and 2 hours to produce a kg of pork, regardless of which family produces it. Suppose the currency unit is Japanese yen, and that the

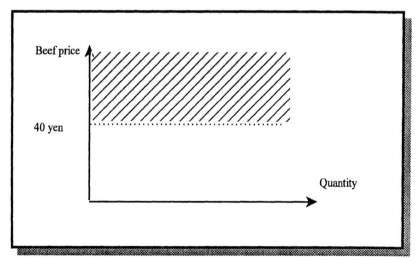

Figure 1.6   Area Acceptable to Beef Seller

average labor cost, in terms of the yen, is 10 yen per labor hour. This is a competitive market, and all exchange happens at equilibrium. Carrying over the above information, we create the following model. Assume Mr. Wang only produces beef and Mr. Zhang only produces pork.

Table 1. 10   Market Model 5

	Beef (Wang)	Pork (Zhang)
Labor hours to produce a kg of meat	4	2
Price /kg of meat	40 yen	20 yen

At what price do Mr. Wang and Mr. Zhang exchange their produce? Mr. Wang wants to get pork from market exchange, and wants to sell beef for at lest 40 yen per kg. Any higher than 40 yen per kg, he will make a profit. Mr. Wang knows it takes him 4 hours of work to produce

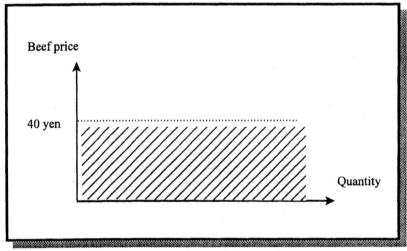

Figure 1.7   Acceptable Trade Area for Beef Buyer

1 kg of beef, and his labor is worth 10 yen per hour. In other words, he can produce other goods and make at least 10 yen per hour. Because the "invisible hand" will move the price of the goods to the labor value

necessary to reproduce the goods, the market price for beef will be 40 yen per kg. Thus, Mr. Wang sells his beef at 40 yen per kg.

If Mr. Wang were to raise pigs, it would cost him 2 hours of labor for 1 kg of pork, half the labor needed to produce the same amount of beef. So he knows that if he were to produce pork it would cost him 20 yen per kg. Therefore, he will only pay 20 yen per kilogram for pork. He certainly does not want to be short-changed.

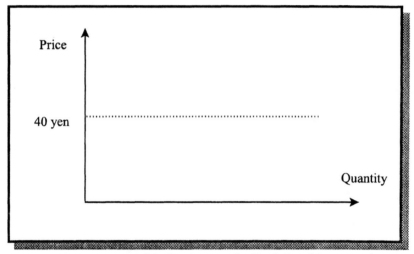

Figure 1.8   Acceptable Trade Area for Both Beef Buyer and Seller

For similar reasons, Mr. Zhang will sell at least 20 yen per kg of pork. Although Mr. Zhang wants to sell at a higher price, he will only be able to sell at 20 yen per kg. The shaded area in Figure 1.6 represents the area in which the beef seller wants to trade. While the shaded area in Figure 1.7 represents the area in which the buyer wants to trade. The only area that is acceptable to both seller and buyer of beef is the horizontal straight line illustrated in Figure 1.8.

THE VALUE OF MONEY

The above market model analysis leads us to ask how the value of money is determined. Why is 10 yen in the above example equal to one hour of socially necessary labor? When gold and silver were used as money, the socially necessary labor used to produce the gold and silver determined the value of the gold and silver. This is the same way in which the value of other goods is determined. Of course, the price of gold and silver is also subject to the change of supply and demand. That is to say, the price of gold and silver will fluctuate around the equilibrium, the socially necessary labor to produce it. The price of the metal will fluctuate when there is a change in the quantity supplied or demanded, even when there is no change in the socially necessary labor needed to produce it. When gold or silver is used as currency, the price of a commodity is subject to the change in quantity supplied and demanded for both the metal itself and the commodity in concern. Gold and silver are no longer used as currency today. Paper money is the standard currency for all countries. The value of paper money is not determined by the socially necessary labor required to produce it. Why? The equilibrium point of commodity exchange equals the value of the socially necessary labor of the commodity in concern only when there is a perfect market. A $100 bill may cost only $1 to produce in mass quantity. But it is not exchanged at the value at the market because its production is monopolized by the U.S. government. This means that no one else is allowed to make U.S. currency; only the government can make it. Private enterprises cannot switch to currency production at will, unlike the production of other commodities, to profit from making currency. The U.S. government does not make currency for profit maximization. The treasury purposely limits the circulation of the currency in order to maintain its value. Because of all these reasons, the value of paper money is maintained and will not be made to equal the socially necessary labor to produce it.

CONCLUSION OF MARKET MODEL 5

The introduction of money does not change the nature of the market. The difference between a barter market and a nonbarter market is that in a nonbarter market, money is used to measure the value of a commodity; while in a barter market, the value of a commodity is measured by the other commodity this commodity can exchange for.

The reason the value of paper currency is higher than the socially necessary labor hours needed to produce it is because the government monopolizes the production of the paper currency. The government purposefully limits the supply of paper currency in order to maintain its value.

DISCUSSION OF ASSUMPTION 1

"Each participant can switch to and from one trade to the other, such as switching from producing beef to pork. There is no restriction in switching between the production of the different goods. The producer can decide what to produce, when, where, how, and what quality to produce. There is also free entry to production, and free flow of the factors of production, and consumption. Each producer also has information on other producers."

The word "participant" refers to a producer of goods. In a market economy, businesses have no restriction in switching from the production of one kind of good to another. This condition is important for proper functioning of the market. Under such conditions, can a business pursue profit by following the market signals of price changes? This producer behavior is the essence of the market mechanism. In addition, all producers in the market can decide at what quantity to produce and at what quality, as well as when and how the merchandise should be produced. Only when these conditions exist can the "invisible hand" function. Factors of production include the factors used in production such as labor, material, physical capital, financial capital, technological information, business information, management information, etc. "Factors of consumption" refers to the conditions where consumers have the freedom to travel, obtain complete information about products or services, and decide when, where, what and at what quantity to purchase products and services. For example, there is a beautiful island that has been developed as a summer resort with hotels, swimming pools, and entertainment. Consumers must have the freedom to travel to this island for consumption.

LAW OF PERFECT MARKETS

Equal exchange of value is a rule for a perfect market. The value of a commodity is determined by the socially necessary labor needed to reproduce it. When two goods exchange hands, they are exchanged with equal value. Since both the buyer and the seller want the best possible exchange, they will only agree to exchange goods at the point which the buyer's payment and the seller's goods have the same value. When goods are exchanged according to the equal exchange of value, the economic resources can be optimally allocated. Equal exchange of value only refers to the equilibrium point.

MARKET MODEL 6 (CAPITAL INVESTMENT IN SINGLE COMMODITY)

In the first market model above, there is no capital. In this section we will try to answer the question: What will happen when capital is introduced? We will discuss the assumption 6 of Market Model 1, which states: "Production is comprised of labor only. It does not include capital and other material costs. It is static, and does not incorporate changes, such as improvement of productivity over time. It does not take time into consideration at all."

The introduction of capital into the analysis is the most difficult part of any theory of value. When capital is introduced into the economy, two things happen. First, how is the return on capital determined? Second, when the laborer is separated from the capital, the laborer no longer owns the capital invested in the production process. What happens to wages?

What is capital? Capital is the money or wealth invested into a production process or business in order to make a profit in the process of improving efficiency, productivity, and production capability. The difference between money and capital is that money spent turns into consumer goods and services, whereas capital invested is intended to bring more wealth. Capital turns into goods and services consumed not by consumers, but by the production process itself. Investors expect returns on the capital, which come in the form of interest, dividends, stock appreciation, or profit.

Suppose there are two fishermen, Mr. Hunter and Mr. Nelson. Each of them can catch 5 fish a day using 5 hours of work on their own, without using any tools. After saving enough food, Mr. Nelson spends 10 hours to make a fishnet. Then, Mr. Nelson invests his net in Mr. Hunter's fishing operation. Mr. Hunter is then able to catch 150 fish a day with only 5 hours of work. Suppose, the net lasts only one day. Among the 150 fish he catches, how many are the result of the fishnet, and how many are the result of the Mr. Hunter's direct labor input? The essential question: How much return would the capitalist Mr. Nelson get from his investment?

Suppose the whole economy is represented by this one commodity and two fishermen society. We will next apply the first law of perfect market - the concept of equal exchange of value.

The fishnet took Mr. Nelson 10 hours to make, so the total return on the capital, including the principle of the investment, should equal 10 hours of labor. The productivity change that results from the introduction of the fishnet can be obtained by comparing fish caught per hour before and after the use of a fishnet.

Fish caught per hour before the net was made
= 5 fish/5 hours = 1 fish/hour

A fisherman can only catch 5 fish in one day (5 hours of work), before the introduction of the fishnet. The value of the labor per hour is equivalent to one fish.

Fish caught per hour after the net is made
= 150 fish/15 = 10 fish/hour

The fisherman Mr. Hunter can catch 150 fish with help of the fishnet Mr. Nelson made. The total labor hours used in the production of the 150 fish is 10 hours needed to produce the fishnet, plus the 5 hours of labor used directly with the fishnet to catch fish. After the introduction of the net, productivity increases. The labor value per hour is equivalent to 10 fish/hour.

It takes 10 hours to make the fishnet. According to the law of equal exchange of value, the investor of the fishnet would also be compensated with 10 hours of labor value, which includes the principal of his investment. After the introduction of fishnet, the one hour of labor can catch 10 fish, thus, the fishnet worth of 10 hours of labor is equivalent to 100 fish. (The total return, including principal, is 10 fish x 10 hrs = 100 fish.) The cost of the net is 10 hours at 1 fish /hour = 10 fish. At the time when the fishnet was made, one hour of labor could only produce 1 fish per hour. The investment has 10 times of return with principle included. (100 fish/10 fish = 10 = 1000%). The net return on investment is 900% (total return/investment - 1 = 100/10 -1 = 9 = 900%).

The 5 hours of labor will produce 10 fish/hour × 5 = 50 fish. Thus, the productivity of the fisherman has increased from 1 fish/hour to 10 fish/hour. That is, the current productivity of labor is 10 times (1000%)

as productive as the labor before the introduction of the fishnet. The productivity growth rate of labor is:

productivity after fishnet/productivity before fishnet - 1
= 100 fish per hour/10 fish per hour - 1
= 10 - 1 = 9 = 900%

Comparing the results between productivity growth rate of labor and net return on investment, we discover that they are equal (Table 1.11). This fact is stated in an equation below:

productivity growth rate of labor = net return on investment

Because:
total return on investment (%) = net return on investment (%) + 1
Therefore:
Total rate of the return on capital (%) (includes principal) - 1
= productivity growth rate of labor

After the fishnet is introduced, productivity increases from 1 fish per hour to 10 fish per hour. To continue production, assume that the fisherman Mr. Hunter obtains a second fishnet from Mr. Nelson. This fishnet also took Mr. Nelson 10 hours to make. Again, the 5 hours of Mr. Hunter's labor plus 10 hours of Mr. Nelson's labor used to make the fishnet can produce 150 fish.

Table 1. 11

Item	Before	After
Productivity	1 fish/labor hour	10 fish/labor hour
Fishnet	10 labor hours =10 fish	10 labor hours =100 fish
Direct labor	5 labor hours = 5 fish	5 labor hours = 50 fish

Since it takes 10 hours to make the fishnet, the total return on the fishnet investment is 10 fish x 10 hours = 100 fish. The cost of the net is 10 hours at 10 fish/hour = 100 fish, since at the time the second fishnet is made, the productivity has become 10 fish/hour due to the introduction of the first fishnet. The fishnet investment has a 100% return. The 5 hours of labor will result in 10 fish/hour x 5 = 50 fish. The productivity of the fisherman has remained the same as 10 fish/hour since the fishnet was originally introduced. In other words, productivity is increased when the first fishnet is introduced, but there is no productivity improvement when the second fishnet is introduced.

In the above, we examine three periods of production. They are illustrated in Table 1.12.

Table 1. 12

Period	1	2	3
Productivity	1 fish/hour	10 fish/hour	10 fish/hour
Productivity growth rate		900%	0%

CONCLUSION OF MARKET MODEL 6

Only when capital investment produces an increase in productivity, will it have a total return (including principal) larger than 100%. When there is no productivity improvement, time alone does not generate a profit or a return, in addition to the investment. In Table 1.12, we examine the three periods to see how the return on capital changes. Notice that from Period Two to Period Three, there is no profit on the investment. The profit is the net return on investment.

productivity growth rate of labor = net return (%) on investment

Because:

total return on investment (%) = net return on investment (%) + 1

Therefore:

Total rate of the return on capital (%) (includes principal) - 1
= productivity growth rate of labor

MARKET MODEL 7 (CAPITAL WITH DUAL COMMODITIES)

In this section we will continue our discussion of assumption 6 of Market Model 1 by introducing currency and additional commodities in order to study how the market works with the introduction of capital.

When there are two or more commodities in the economy, the case becomes more complex. Next, I will introduce a second commodity and third producer into the fisherman story. Suppose that there is a third producer, Mr. Wheeler, who produces wheat. No improvement has been made on the production of wheat, so the productivity of wheat has not changed. Suppose an economy consists of only two fishermen and a wheat producer. Everything else remains the same.

Suppose a fisherman can catch 5 fish a day with 5 hours of work without using any tools. After saving enough food, he spends 10 hours to make a fishnet. He is then able to catch 150 fish per day with 5 hours of work. Also, the fishnet will only last one day. Among the 150 fish he catches, how many are the return on the fishnet, and how many result from the fisherman's direct labor input? The essential question: how much return could the capitalist get from his investment?

Apply the equal exchange of value as we discussed above. Suppose the whole economy includes only three persons: fisherman Mr. Hunter, a wheat producer Mr. Wheeler, and Mr. Nelson.

Since the fishnet took Mr. Nelson 10 hours to make, the total return on the capital, including the principal of the investment, should equal 10 hours of labor. This productivity change that results from the introduction of the fishnet can be represented with fish caught per hour.

Fish caught per hour before the net made = 5 fish/5 hours = 1 fish/hour. The fisherman Mr. Hunter can only catch 5 fish with one day of 5 hours of work. Before the introduction of the fishnet, one labor hour is equivalent to 1 fish/hour.

Productivity per hour after the net is made is 150 fish/15 = 10 fish/hour. The fisherman, Mr. Hunter, can catch 150 fish using the fishnet Mr. Nelson made. The total labor hours used in the production of these 150 fish is the 10 hours needed to produce the fishnet plus the 5 hours of labor used directly with the fishnet. After the introduction of the fishnet, productivity increases; one labor hour is now equivalent to 10 fish/hour.

It takes 10 hours to make the fishnet. The total return is 10 fish × 10 hours = 100 fish. The cost of the net is 10 hours at 1 fish /hour = 10 fish. The fishnet investment has a 1000% return (including the principal). The 5 hours of labor will produce 10 fish/hour x 5 = 50 fish. The productivity of the fisherman has increased from producing 1 fish/hour to 10 fish/hour.

Suppose each fish can be sold for $1 in Period 1 and $0.30 in Period 2. The productivity is 1 fish per hour in Period 1, and 10 fish/hour in Period 2. The price drops because of the increase in supply. This increase causes the price to decrease under normal circumstances. Suppose that one socially necessary labor is equivalent to $1.00.

The total revenue per day, before the introduction of the fishnet, is $5.00 for the fisherman, Mr. Hunter. The revenue of 5 hours of labor, after the introduction of the fishnet, is $0.30 × 10 × 5 = $15.00 (price of fish x total catch in 5 hours) That is $3.00 earning per labor hour. When this happens, more labor and capital will be attracted to the fishing industry, and the price of fish will drop until there is no further gain in switching from one trade (wheat) to another (fishing). That is, the wheat producer will spend more time on fishing and reduce the hours spent on producing wheat activity. When an equilibrium point is reached, the fishing labor will be compensated at the same rate as the other trade (wheat growing). Everything else remains the same. This includes the hardship of producing fish or wheat. The capital good here is the fishnet. The return on the capital (including the principal) is 300% ($15.00/$5.00 =300%). The return will drop to 100% over time as more and more capital moves into fishing in a perfect capital market. Table 1.13 summarizes the changes.

When we apply the rule of equal exchange value, we find that if a capitalist, Mr. Nelson, invests in the fishnet valued at 10 labor hours in Period 1, he should get 10 labor hours back that are equivalent to 100 fish or $10 in Period 3 where equilibrium has been achieved. The capitalist makes more money during the transitory Period 2 before the price falls back to the labor value of the fish. Therefore, the surplus value is only transitory and occurs before the market reaches a new equilibrium. Once the market reaches the new equilibrium, there is no more profit. Transitory profit happens when there is a productivity improvement over the previous period. However, the capitalists' pursuit of profit promotes the productivity improvement and eventually benefits society as a whole.

This two-commodity example only illustrates the change of return on the capital of a particular commodity. It does not provide a relationship between productivity, capital, or return on capital, since it only studies a particular case, not a general case. Being focused on a particular case, it does not study the average return on capital. As I discussed earlier, we do not want to study the price change, since prices can be set randomly high

Table 1. 13

Item	Period 1, no fishnet	Period 2, with fishnet	Period 3, reach equilibrium
Price of fish	$1.00	$0.30	$0.1
One labor hour	1 fish = $1	10 fish = $3	10 fish = $1
Productivity compared with previous period		1000%	100%
5 hours direct labor	5 fish = $5	50 fish = $15	50 fish = $5
Capital, 10 labor hours =	10 fish = $10	100 fish = $30	100 fish = $10

or low. We study the core-- the value of goods, around which price fluctuates up and down with the change of supply and demand. To study the average return on capital, we study the following case where return on capital represents the average of the economy.

CONCLUSION OF MARKET MODEL 7

Surplus value is only transitory and occurs before the market reaches a new equilibrium. Once the market reaches the new equilibrium, there is no more surplus value. Transitory surplus value happens when there is a productivity improvement over the previous period. However, the capitalists' pursuit of profit promotes the productivity improvement and eventually benefits society as a whole.

MARKET MODEL 8 (THE MODEL FOR AVERAGE CAPITAL BEHAVIOR)

This section will introduce currency and inflation. The objective of this section is to study the market in order to discover the relationships among major economic parameters, such as profit rate, interest rate, inflation rate, and productivity growth rate. ("Productivity improvement rate" and "productivity growth rate" have the same meaning.)

Suppose we have a perfect competitive market. There are many producers who use his or her labor to produce commodities. Some of them use capital goods made by themselves or obtained from the market. In this case, capital and laborer have not been separated. Suppose the economy experiences a 5% productivity improvement from year 100 to year 101. Suppose Mr. Shoemaker is a typical shoe producer whose productivity changes represent the average economic improvement. Suppose Mr. Shoemaker can only produce 300 pairs of shoes during a normal year, without any capital goods in the year 100. Suppose he obtains a steel shoe machine from an investor, Mr. Smith, who has spent one year of labor to make the shoe machine. In the year 101, Mr. Shoemaker used the shoe machine to improve his production. The use of shoe machine made a 5% productivity improvement. Productivity improvement is measured by comparing the output per labor hours of input before and after the use of the shoe machine. The labor hours of input include direct and indirect labor input. The indirect labor input is the shoe machine, which has past labor hours embedded in it. Suppose for the sake of simplicity, that the shoe machine can only last one year. The shoe machine needs one man to operate it, which is equivalent to two people working together to make shoes. The shoe machine can be thought of as just like another person, except that it brings productivity improvement.

Suppose that in the year 101, Mr. Shoemaker made $(300 + 300) \times 1.05 = 630$ pairs of shoes with the assistance of the shoe machine. (600 represents two laborer's yearly output, and 1.05 represents a 5% productivity improvement.) The 630 pairs of shoes are made by two years of labor. One year is the direct labor from Mr. Shoemaker and the other year is Mr. Smith's labor, embedded in the machine. At the end of the year 101, Mr. Shoemaker will pay back the maker of the machine the equivalent of one year's work, because Mr. Smith demanded that he get at least the one year of labor that he invested in the machine. Mr. Smith wants more, but under competitive market conditions, he can only exchange goods at the exact value of the goods. Measured by the number of shoes, Mr. Smith would get 315 pairs of shoes (630/2 = 315 pairs of shoes) back at the end of the year 101. That is 5% more than 300 pairs of shoes. The 300 pairs of shoes are the equivalent of one year of labor in the year 100. The difference between 315 pairs and 300 pairs is the profit on the capital.

When there is no inflation or deflation, the price of goods stays the same. Assume that a pair of shoes can be sold for $10. The price did not change from year 100 to year 101. Mr. Smith's shoe machine is worth 300 pairs of shoes in year 100, equivalent to $3000. In year 101, Mr. Smith receives $3150 as total payment, equivalent to 315 pairs of shoes. The $150 difference is Mr. Smith's profit on his investment. Meanwhile, Mr. Shoemaker also benefits from Mr. Smith's investment, because Mr. Shoemaker's earning also increased from $3000 per year to $3150 per year. The profit rate equals profit/investment. In this case, Mr. Smith's profit rate is $150/$3000 = 5%.

From these examples, we can conclude that the average profit rate on capital is equal to the productivity improvement rate of the economy, provided that there is no inflation or deflation in price.

When there is inflation, the average profit rate on capital can be expressed as below. Please note that all the factors we study here are averages. They are an inflation rate, profit rate, and productivity growth rate. The price change on the shoes represents the average price change of the economy.

In order to obtain a general equation, we use variables in Table 1.14. In the first row of table is the period. Before the introduction of capital is the first period, after the introduction of the capital is the second period. TL represents total labor in the first period. In the second period, total input is doubled. It includes the labor hours embedded in the shoe machine. Price level of shoes in the first period is $P(0)$. Inflation rate is I. The price of shoes changes at the same rate as the consumer inflation rate of the economy. Therefore, the shoe price level is $P(0)(1 + I)$. Total output in the first period is Q. In the second period, the output would be 2Q without the productivity improvement, since the input doubled. S is the productivity growth rate of the economy, and the shoemaking industry has the same speed of productivity growth rate. The total output of the second period is $2Q(1 + S)$. Total revenue = price × total output.

Total capital investment for Period 2 is TL in labor hours.

Because of the law of equal exchange of value, the total capital input of the second period equals the part of the revenue of the second period generated by capital in terms of labor hours. Thus, we have:

Table 1. 14

Period	1	2
Total labor Input	TL	2TL
Price	P(0)	P(0)(1 + I)
Total output	Q	2Q(1 + S)
Total Revenue	P(0)Q	P(0)(1 + I) × 2Q(1 + S)

TL equivalent to P(0)Q

(At the beginning of the second period, productivity is the same as in Period 1. Thus, the input of the second period can be expressed by the above expression.)

The profit rate of the second period can be expressed as:
(Direct labor input is TL and indirect labor input (shoe machine) is TL. The total is 2TL. Only half of 2TL is capital, therefore only half of the total revenue in Period 2 is the capital share of total revenue.)

Profit rate = (capital share of total revenue)/(capital investment) - 1
            = P(0)(1 + I) × Q(1 + S) /P(0)Q - 1
            = (1 + I)(1 + S) - 1
         let P = profit rate
         We have:
         P + 1 = (1 + I)(1 + S)
Where:
         P: profit rate
         I: inflation rate
         S: productivity growth rate

For example, the price of a pair of shoes increases 10% from year 100 to year 101. That is, the price of a pair of shoes moves upward from

$10 to $11. Mr. Smith's one year of labor in the year 100 would stay the same as $3000. The same one year of labor will be equal to 315 pairs of shoes in the year 101. At the price of $11, the 315 pairs of shoes will amount to $3465. The profit rate is $3465/$3000 = 15.5%

We can also calculate by using this equation:

$$P + 1 = (1 + I)(1 + S)$$
Average profit rate = $P = (1 + 5\%)(1 + 10\%) - 1 = 15.5\%$

The profit on an investment in the shoe making machine can also be thought of as an interest rate. Instead of investing the shoemaking machine in Mr. Shoemaker's business, Mr. Smith can loan Mr. Shoemaker capital, which is equivalent to one year of labor. Mr. Shoemaker can then purchase a machine from Mr. Smith or from another vendor in the market. Mr. Shoemaker then returns the capital, with interest, to Mr. Smith at the end of the period. From a theoretical point of view, profit and interest are actually the same thing. They come from the same source and follow the same rules. However, profit and interest in the modern economy fall under different definitions, and therefore, they carry different risks. When we deposit money in a bank, the bank promises an interest rate. The risk associated with this action is much smaller than investing money in a business. This is why government bonds and treasury bills carry less earning power than the stock market. If we assume a perfect world where the risk is zero, then we can easily see that the interest rate should be equal to the profit rate. Interest and profit are just different ways of looking at the same thing.

Average Profit Rate = Average Interest Rate when risk is zero.

Or when risk is zero,

$$P = (1 + I)(1 + S) - 1 = \text{Average interest rate}$$
$$P = (1 + S)(1 + I) - 1 = R$$
$$P = R = (1 + S)(1 + I) - 1$$
$$P + 1 = R + 1 = (1 + S)(1 + I)$$

Where:

P: average profit rate
S: productivity growth rate

I: inflation rate
R: Average interest rate

Recall that all numbers are averages. In the real world, there are risks associated with everything. Sometimes, people lose everything they invest in a business. Other times, the bank never gets anything back from the loan it grants. For these reasons, the real world average profit rate and the average interest rate are higher than what is expressed above. In the above equation, when the productivity growth rate is zero and inflation is zero, we have zero for average profit rate and the average interest rate. This is inconceivable, since no one will make a loan or investment without expecting some return in addition to the principal. The profit or interest is determined by the risk involved, transaction cost, and the supply and demand for capital. The productivity growth rate in the above equation refers to the average social productivity growth rate of an economy, not that of a particular manufacturer, or retailer. The inflation rate refers to the average rise in price level in an economy.

Similarly to the average profit rate, the average labor wage rate will increase at the same rate. This may appear to be accidental, but it is not. Regardless of what the ratio is between direct labor input and capital input in the production process, we have (Table 1.14):

labor compensation increase rate
= direct labor compensation in Period 2/ direct labor compensation in Period 1 - 1
$= P(0)(1 + I)Q(1 + S)/P(0)Q = (1 + I)(1 + S) - 1$

(Note: Only half of the total revenue in Period 2 is generated by direct labor, while all revenue in Period 1 is generated by direct labor. According to the law of equal exchange of value, the laborer would get the same amount of compensation as the labor hours used in production.)

$$L = (1 + S)(1 + I) - 1$$
Where:
L: average wage rate increase
S: productivity growth rate
I: inflation rate

For example, the price of a pair of shoes increases 10% from year 100 to year 101. That is, the price of a pair of shoes moves upward from $10 to $11. Mr. Shoemaker's one year of labor in year 100 would be the same as $3000. The same one year of labor will be equal to 315 pairs of shoes in the year 101. At the price of $11, the 315 pairs of shoes will amount to $3465. The wage increase rate is ($3465 - $3000)/$3000 =$465/$3000 = 15.5%

$$L = (1 + 5\%) \times (1 + 10\%) - 1 = 15.5\%$$

CONCLUSION OF MARKET MODEL 8

Under perfect market conditions, at equilibrium, when the producer enjoys the same productivity growth rate as the average productivity growth rate of the economy and when the price of goods concerned increases at the same speed as the inflation rate of the economy, we have the following relations:

$$(1 + L) = (1 + P) = (1 + R) = (1 + S)(1 + I) \qquad (1.4)$$

Where:

L: labor compensation increase rate
P: profit rate of the producer
R: interest rate
S: productivity growth rate of either producer or economy
I: inflation rate

Alternatively, the above equations can be expressed as:

$$P = (1 + S)(1 + I) - 1$$
$$L = (1 + S)(1 + I) - 1$$
$$R = (1 + S)(1 + I) - 1$$

$$(1.5)$$

Profit and interest are not surplus values in this case. According to Marx, surplus value can only be generated if goods are not exchanged with equal value. In the above analysis, we applied the rule of equal exchange of value, but we still obtained interest and profit. Interest and profit are necessary to the equal exchange of value; therefore, they are necessary for the efficiency of the market economy. Profit and interest are not all evil. They are merely the reflection and result of an improvement in the productivity of an economy.

MARKET MODEL 9 (SEPARATION OF LABOR AND CAPITAL)

In this market model, we study what happens when the capital and laborer are separated.

The above analysis holds true when the production unit is individual or family based. The production unit will maximize their earning, and the individual or family labor in the production are the sole direct labor input. The above examples describe a rudimentary society where the individual is a production unit. The individual's demand for more goods and services results in an equal exchange of value.

In today's modern economy, the format of production has changed. The advancement of technology and engineering makes production more efficient, with the employment of more and more capital stocks, such as machines and technological goods used for production. The laborer no longer directly owns the capital. The investors own the capital, and they are seeking the highest possible return on their investment. Under this arrangement of separation of capital from labor, managers of the production unit (businesses or corporations) will push workers' compensation as low as possible in order to maximize profit. When this happens, the equation above will change to the following partial equation. (This can happen when the economy does not have full employment.)

$$P \geq (1 + S)(1 + I) - 1$$
$$L \leq (1 + S)(1 + I) - 1$$
$$R \geq (1 + S)(1 + I) - 1$$

Where:

P: average profit rate
L: average wage rate increase
S: productivity growth rate
I: inflation rate

Thus the capitalist or business owner will enjoy a higher than average profit rate, while the average wage rate increase of workers is lower. The analysis below illustrates where the equilibrium is under two conditions: full employment and less than full employment.

This model illustrates a special case where the productivity growth rate of the producer is the same as the average productivity growth rate of society. In the next model a more general case will be presented.

Suppose we have a perfect competitive market. There are many producers who use his or her labor to produce commodities. Some of them use capital goods made by themselves or obtained from the market. In this case, the capital and laborer have not been separated. In other words, individuals work for themselves, and labor is not hired. Suppose the economy experiences a 20% productivity improvement from year 200 to year 201, and Mr. Shoemaker is a typical shoe producer whose productivity change represents the average economic improvement. Mr. Shoemaker can only produce 300 pairs of shoes during a normal year, without any capital goods in the year 200. There are many shoemakers like Mr. Shoemaker. Mr. Smith is the shoe machine inventor and manufacturer. Some shoemakers were able to obtain a steel shoe machine from a machine producer like Mr. Smith who has spent one year of labor to make the shoe machine.

In the year 201, Mr. Shoemaker used the steel shoe machine to improve his production. Consequently, his productivity improved 20%. The productivity is measured by considering all input in terms of labor hours, which includes direct and indirect input of labor hour. Indirect labor hour is embedded in the machine. Suppose the shoe machine can only last one year, and it takes two people to operate the shoe machine. This is equivalent to 3 people working together to make shoes. The shoe machine can be thought of as just like another person, except that it brings productivity improvement. In the year 201, Mr. Shoemaker made 900 x 1.20 = 1080 pairs of shoes with the assistance of the shoe machine and hired labor. (900 represents three laborer's yearly output, and 1.20 represents a 20% productivity improvement). These 1080 pairs of shoes consist of three years of labor. One is the direct labor from Mr. Shoemaker; one is the hired labor of Mr. Workman; and the third is Mr. Smith's labor, embedded within the shoe machine. At the end of the year 201, Mr. Shoemaker will pay back Mr. Smith, the machine maker, the equivalent of one year of work. This is because Mr. Smith demanded that he get at least his one year of labor returned, since the shoe machine cost

Mr. Smith one year of labor to make, Mr. Smith wants more money in return, but under competitive market conditions where Mr. Smith is not the sole producer of the shoe machine, Mr. Smith can only exchange goods at the value of the goods. If measured by the number of shoes, Mr. Smith would get 360 pairs of shoes (1080 /3 = 360 pairs of shoes) at the end of year 201, or 20% more than 300 pairs of shoes. The 300 pairs of shoes are the equivalent of one year of labor in the year 200. The difference between the 360 pairs and the 300 pairs is the profit on the capital.

The transaction between Mr. Shoemaker and Mr. Smith is regulated by the market, and is confined to an equal exchange of value. The transaction between Mr. Shoemaker and Mr. Workman is not. For a variety of possible reasons, Mr. Workman chooses to work for Mr. Shoemaker, because Mr. Shoemaker promises to pay him more than he can make on his own, which is 300 pairs of shoes a year by himself. Suppose Mr. Shoemaker reaches a deal with Mr. Workman in which Mr. Shoemaker will pay him the equivalent of 310 pairs of shoes a year for his labor in the year 201. The total production in the year 201 is 1080 pairs of shoes, minus the payment of 360 pairs to Mr. Smith and 310 pairs to Mr. Workman, is what Mr. Shoemaker made (1080 − 360 − 310 = 410). While an average labor should have made 360 pairs of shoes, Mr. Shoemaker made 410 pairs of shoes with only one year of labor. On average, he should get 360 pairs of shoes. The 50 pairs of shoes he made above the 360 pairs is surplus value.

The more laborers there are available on the market, the more power Mr. Shoemaker has to negotiate lower wages for his workers. As others see how quickly Mr. Shoemaker becomes rich, they will start businesses like his. Two things may happen.

First, the wage may stay the same if there is a sufficient labor supply, as this is true for most of the world today. Mr. Shoemakers' surplus value, measured in money, will decline resulting from the competition which drives the price of shoes down. The surplus value will eventually reach zero, at least in theory. In reality, however, the decline of surplus value will probably not reach zero for several reasons. These costs include the difficulty involved in getting into the business, industrial monopolies or oligopolies, and the fact that capitalists are able to push wages down.

However, in perfect market conditions under full employment, the market mechanism will move the surplus value toward zero. In other words, there is no surplus value in equilibrium in a perfect competitive market when there is full employment.

Secondly, if the supply of labor is limited, wages may be driven up by more demand for labor, since shoemaking is so profitable. Eventually, Mr. Shoemaker's surplus value will decrease until it reaches zero, at least in theory, provided that there is always a market for the product. Because the labor supply is always plentiful in the real world, it is often easy for capitalists to control the rate of wage increases. However, if we suppose that the labor supply is limited and fixed, then we can confidently predict the surplus value Mr. Shoemaker previously enjoyed will decline. As one business hires employees away from another business, wages are driven up during the process until no more gain can be made.

CONCLUSION OF MARKET MODEL 9

The above analysis suggests the following conclusions.

1. When the economy does not have full employment and laborer is separated from capital, we have the following:

    $P \geq (1 + S)(1 + I) - 1$

    $R \geq (1 + S)(1 + I) - 1$

    $L \leq (1 + S)(1 + I) - 1$

2. When the economy has full employment and laborer is separated from capital, we have the following:

    $P = (1 + S)(1 + I) - 1$

    $L = (1 + S)(1 + I) - 1$

Where:

      P: average profit rate

      L: average wage rate increase

      S: productivity growth rate

      I: inflation rate

MARKET MODEL 10 (PRODUCER PRODUCTIVITY DIFFERS FROM THAT OF THE ECONOMY, FULL EMPLOYMENT)

We will now examine full employment situations where the producer may not enjoy the same productivity growth rate as the average productivity growth rate of the whole economy. The objective of this analysis is to answer the following questions under the condition that the laborer is separated from capital: Is there any surplus value at equilibrium? Does the equilibrium wage uphold the equal exchange of value rule? What happens to equilibrium prices?

Model 10 (Full Employment Equilibrium under deflation)(Table 1.15) is a competitive market with full employment. We will examine a lobster producer, Mr. Fisher.

Row 1. There are four periods in this model. In the first period, there is no capital stock (machines or tools); direct labor is the only input for production. In the second period, capital stock (tools) is introduced; and consequently, productivity improves. The laborer is separated from capital. The capitalists or investors own the tools of production. Labor is hired to produce the lobsters. Capitalists and investors enjoy surplus value in Periods 2 and 3, which attracts more investment and labor into the business.   The production expands. The result is Period Three. As production expands, more products are put into the market and price falls until it reaches a new equilibrium. This new equilibrium is the fourth period.

Row 2. Direct labor, in the second Row, records the average socially necessary labor used in production. Remember in the first period, the laborer works for himself. From the second period on, the laborers work for the capitalists or investors. The amount of socially necessary labor is measured by the average hours.

Row 3. The third row represents capital (capital stock), which is the tools or machinery used in production. It is recorded in terms of the socially necessary labor hours needed to produce the capital stock. Only the realized capital is shown, not the total principal value of the machine. For example, a machine costs 100 labor hours, and can only produce 200 lobsters. If only 100 lobsters are produced, then the realized capital is only half the value of the machine, or 50 labor hours.

Row 4. This row represents the quantity of the product produced. The quantity will be the number of lobsters produced.

Row 5. Cost per product is a different way of measuring productivity in terms of the average socially necessary labor hours needed to produce, for example, one lobster. This is calculated by dividing the total quantity of the product by the total amount of direct and indirect labor used, which is the sum of the row 2 (direct labor) and row 3 (capital). Here, cost decreased from Period 1 to Period 2 because productivity improvement machinery is introduced. There is no cost change from Period 2 to Period 4.

Row 6. Wages refers to the compensation to the laborer. It is

Table 1. 15   Market Model 10

1	Period	1	2	3	4
2	Direct labor (hr)	100	100	400	500
3	Capital (hr)	0	100	400	500
4	Output (Q)	100	300	1200	1500
5	Cost (hr)	1	0.67	0.67	0.67
6	Wages (hr)	100	≥ 100	>400	500
7	Wages ($)	$100	$\geq\$100$	>$400	$500
8	Return to the capitalists (hr)	0	>100	>400	500
9	Monetary return on capital ($)	0	>$100	>$400	$500
10	Price of lobster ($)	$1	$1> x >0.67$	$x>y>0.67$	0.67
11	Lobsters per hour	1	1.5	1.5	1.5
12	Total Revenue ($)	$100	$300>x>201$	$1200>x>801$	1000

measured by average social labor hours. The numbers presented for the first and the fourth periods are the equilibrium point. The numbers in the second and third periods are transitory numbers. In an economy, if an average labor hour produces 10 fish per hour, but only gets paid 5 fish per hour, we say that the labor is paid 0.5 labor hours for each labor hour of work.

Row 7. Wages in dollar amount is monetary compensation to labor. It is found by converting row 6, from labor hours to monetary terms. In this model, we assume that $1.00 is equivalent to one labor hour in all

4 periods of time.

Row 8. Return to the capitalist is measured in the average socially necessary labor hours. The numbers presented for the first and the fourth periods are the equilibrium points. The numbers in the second and third periods are the transitory numbers. At equilibrium, the investor gets exactly what was invested in terms of average socially necessary labor hours.

Row 9. Monetary return on capital is found by converting return to the capitalist (row 8) from labor hours to monetary terms. In this model, $1.00 is equivalent to one average labor hour.

Row 10. The price of lobster is obtained from the cost per product in labor hours (row 5). When we covert row 5 from labor hours to monetary terms ($1/labor hour × row 5), we get the equilibrium price, such as in Periods 1 and 4. In Periods 2 and 3, the price is in transitory state. Its possible range is limited by the cost per product (row 5).

Row 11. Lobsters per hour is an indicator of productivity. The more lobster that can be produced per labor hour, the higher the productivity is. This is calculated by dividing the quantity of the product (row 4) by the sum of the direct labor (row 2) and indirect labor (capital) (row 3).

Row 12. Total monetary revenue is the total revenue of the lobster products produced by this one producer. It is determined by multiplying the price of lobster (row 10) and the quantity of product (row 4).

Suppose that in the first period of time, 100 labor hours of direct labor can produce 100 lobsters without using any capital. Such that the cost per lobster is 1 labor hour. At equilibrium, goods are exchanged with equal value; therefore, the compensation to the laborer is 100 labor hours, or $100 in monetary terms. The market price of the lobster is $1 per lobster. The productivity is 1 lobster per average labor hour.

Suppose that in the second period of time, capital is introduced. Remember that "capital" refers to machines that can improve productivity. For every 100 direct labor hours, 100 labor hours of capital will be used. The output increases to 300 lobsters. The cost of each product decreases to 0.67 average labor hours [(100+100)hr /300 lobster = 0.67]. There is a 50% (Row 11, lobsters per hour) productivity improvement in lobster production for Mr. Fisher's business. The economy may be enjoying a 1% to 15% average productivity gain, which is different from productivity growth rate enjoyed by the producer Mr. Fisher. However, Mr. Fisher does not have to increase the wages of his labor force. He can pay the same amount of money they would receive if they worked for themselves. If he is a nice person, Mr. Fisher may decide to give his workers a raise. That is why row 6, Wages (hour) is larger than or equal to 100 hours. Since we assume $1 will be equivalent to 1 labor hour, row 7 will be larger than or equal to $100. Mr. Fisher would naturally expect his capital investment to bring a profit. This is why rows 8 and 9 are larger than 100, which is the amount of capital realized in production. Notice that the sum of total wage hours for the labor and return to capital in labor hours is larger than the amount of direct labor plus capital input into production. This would happen if Mr. Fisher's business is improving its productivity faster than the average productivity growth rate in the lobster industry.

In other words, if on average in the economy it takes 0.95 hours to produce one lobster, the 300 lobsters produced in Period 2 by Mr. Fisher's business will be equivalent to 300 x 0.95 = 285 average socially necessary labor hours. (Please note that the following words may have been used interchangeably, but have the same meaning: average labor hour, socially necessary labor hour, average socially necessary labor hour, labor hour, labor value hour, and labor value.) Thus, in Period Two, an input of 200 labor hours produces an output of 285 labor hours if the social average time needed to produce lobster is 0.95 hours. However, this is a transitory condition. It will not last, because the production increase will lead to a supply increase at the market. The price of lobster will decrease from the original $1 per lobster (row 10, Period 1). The cost of the product is 0.67 hours (see row 5, Period 2). If we convert the 0.67 hours to monetary terms, it is now $0.67, which is the lowest possible price. This suggests the actual price will be between $1 and $0.67 per lobster. This suggests that a large profit can be made by increasing production. A production expansion is illustrated in Period 3.

The number of lobsters produced per hour (row 11) increases from 1 to 1.5 from Period 1 to Period 2. The total revenue is between $300 and $201. To illustrate the profitability in this period, we suppose total revenue is $260 for Period 2, after paying $220 for capital and labor there is still a $40 surplus value left for Mr. Fisher ($220 is an assumed number, we can assume any number that is larger than the sum of row 7 and row 9 in Period 2). However, the surplus value is transitory. (Readers are encouraged to calculate the profit by assuming a different level of revenue between $300 and $201 in order to get a feel for how profitable it is in this period.)

Suppose that in the third period Mr. Fisher expands his business, as did many other lobster producers with the help of machinery. This will happen because investors, business people, and capitalists will relentlessly pursue profit. For Mr. Fisher, direct labor increases from 100 to 400 labor hours, as did the capital. The quantity of product increased from 300 to 1200 lobsters. Cost of product (row 5) stays the same. The total wages for direct labor increase to 400 hours since 400 hours of direct labor are used, and Mr. Fisher will need to pay the monetary equivalent of more than 400 labor hours to the laborers. The reason is that under full employment, laborers will only move from one job to another if one offers better wages. This is why row 7 in Period 3 is larger than or equal to $400. Since capitalist will expect something in return, we, therefore, assume row 8 and row 9 are both larger than 400. The price will fall again from Period 2 level, but it is still higher than $0.67 (row 10). In row 10, the price x is the price level for Period 2, and y is the price level of Period 3. The price in Period 3 is lower than price in Period 2. In Period 3, surplus value still exists. This will attract more businesses, and Mr. Fisher will continue expanding production.

Period 4 presents an equilibrium point. Suppose Mr. Fisher expands his production with direct labor from 400 labor hours to 500 labor hours, as did the machinery (rows 1 and 2 in Period 4), causing total product output to increase from 1200 to 1500 (row 4) lobsters. The cost of the product (row 5) remains the same: 0.67 labor hours. At equilibrium, the price of the product falls back to $0.67 (row 10), the equivalent to the labor necessary to produce the goods. At this price level, the total revenue is $1000. Mr. Fisher wants more for his investment, but if he were to pay his workers less than $1 per labor hour, his workers would leave for other jobs. Thus, he reduces his workers' pay from a level higher than $1 per labor hour in Period 3, to $1 per hour in Period 4. Since he could not pay workers any less, he will pay them a total of $500 (row 7), leaving $500 to repay his investors.

In these 4 steps, we see that before the market returns to its equilibrium point, more surplus value is to be made. When more capital enters the market in search of surplus value, the surplus value decreases until it vanishes. This is a transitory phenomenon. An economy may have several production sectors enjoying productivity improvement and surplus value. As long as there is enough capital to go around, the economic sector that enjoys surplus value will always attract additional business. At equilibrium, surplus value is zero. However, if we look at every labor hour, we will find each labor hour now commands more goods than before. In Period 4, each labor hour is equivalent to 1.5 lobsters, compared with only 1 lobster in Period 1. An investor with $500 will command (1.5 × 500 labor hours =) 750 lobsters in Period 4, compared with 500 lobsters in Period 1. The 500 hours of direct labor input will be rewarded with $500, which can also command 750 lobsters. While in Period 1, 500 labor hours will only be able to command 500 lobsters. In an economy where Mr. Fisher is just one of many producers of a variety of merchandise, some industries may have a productivity improvement where surplus value is created, while other industries may have no productivity improvements and no surplus value created. Capital will move into the industries and businesses where surplus value can be created until it reaches zero. Also, please note in the above example, the average price level of the economy is falling. We know this because we have assumed that $1 = 1 labor hour, and from Period 1 to Period 4, the number of products made by an average labor hour has increased. This is deflation.

CONCLUSION OF MARKET MODEL 10

In a perfect competitive market with full employment, when the producer enjoys a better than social average productivity growth rate, the producer will make transitory surplus value before the price drops back to the level that reflects the socially necessary labor hours needed to produce the product.

There is no surplus value at equilibrium. The equilibrium wage uphold the equal exchange of value rule, in other words, the wages at equilibrium correctly reflect the labor hours input. At equilibrium, price will correctly reflect the socially necessary labor hours needed to produce the product.

There is deflation when the monetary equivalent of one labor hour is held constant.

MARKET MODEL 11 (FULL EMPLOYMENT WITHOUT DEFLATION)

This model is to illustrate what happens when there is no deflation, when the average price movement is zero. The price of some goods may go

Table 1. 16

Time	Start	End
Output per labor hour	100	105
Monetary equivalent per labor hour	$1.00	$1.05
Price of good (row 3 divided by row 2)	$0.01	$0.01

up, while others may go down; but the net effect is zero. Further, we must assume that the average productivity growth rate of the economy in the concerned Periods 1 to 4 is 5%. From this, we know that the previous assumption $1 = 1 labor hour for all four periods must change. Assume that $1 = 1 labor hour in Period 1. It will become $1.05 = 1 labor hour in Period 4.

The following explains why this will happen. Assume that for an average commodity, a particular toy, the average laborer can produce 100 toys per labor hour initially. Because there is a 5% productivity increase of the entire economy in the concerned period, one labor hour will be able to produce 105 toys in the end (Table 1.16). Assume that toy production has the same rate of productivity increase as that of the whole economy.

Because the price is calculated by the following:

price of good
= (one labor hour in monetary term)/(hourly output by labor)

For the start of the period, we have
price of good = $1.00/100 = $0.01

For the end of the period, we have
price of good = $1.05/105 = $0.01

The rate of increase in monetary term per labor hour is thus the same as the average productivity improvement rate of the whole economy in the same period, so there is no inflation or deflation. See Table 1.16.

Table 1.17 illustrates the Periods 1 and 4 of Market Model 10. It shows data for a constant price with full employment. We only need to examine Periods 1 and 4; therefore, columns for Periods 2 and 3 of Model 10 are not reproduced here. A factor of 1.05 is used to multiply any row with a dollar sign in Period 4 of the original table in order to get the new Period 4 dollar amounts in Table 1.17.

Table 1. 17

1	Period	1	4
2	Direct labor (hr)	100	500
3	Capital(hr)	0	500
4	Output (Q)	100	1500
5	Cost (hr)	1	0.67
6	Wages (hr)	100	500
7	Wages ($)	$100	$525
8	Return to the capitalists (hr)	0	500
9	Monetary return on capital ($)	0	$525
10	Price of lobster ($)	$1	$0.70
11	lobsters per hour	1	1.5
12	Total Revenue ($)	$100	$1050

All conditions are the same as discussed in Model 10, except that the price level has zero inflation. The total monetary revenue in Period 4 increases to $1050 from $1000 in the previous deflation model. The price of lobster in Period 4 becomes $0.70 a piece, up from $0.67 in the previous model. Monetary compensation to labor increases to $525 from $500 in the previous as does the return on capital. This is a 5% increase in labor compensation, which is the same as the productivity growth rate of the economy.

CONCLUSION OF MARKET MODEL 11

From this two period table, we can make a few conclusions. In a perfect competitive market with full employment and zero inflation ($I = 0$):

1.   The monetary compensation to labor increases at a rate equal to the average social productivity improvement rate of the economy ($L = S$).

2.   The monetary return to capitalist equals the average social productivity improvement rate of the economy ($P = S$).

3.   The price of goods will fall if production enjoys a higher rate of productivity improvement than that of the general economy. ·

4.   There is no surplus value at equilibrium.

5.   At equilibrium, wage and capital are exchanged by the rule of equal exchange of value.

MARKET MODEL 12   (SALMON MODEL, MARKET WITH UNEMPLOYMENT, WITHOUT INFLATION)

Market Model 12 is essentially identical to the above lobster model (Models 10 and 11), except that full employment does not exist. In other words, there is a significant percentage of unemployment.

The following is a more general case where the producer may not enjoy the same productivity improvement rate as the average rate of the whole economy. The objective of this analysis is to answer the following questions (under the condition that the laborer is separated from capital): Is there any surplus value at equilibrium? Do equilibrium wages uphold the equal exchange of value rule? What happens to equilibrium prices?

In a competitive market, we will examine a salmon producer, Mr. Fujimoto. (See Table 1.18)

Row 1. There are four periods in this model. In the first period, there is no capital stock (machines or tools). The direct labor is the only input for production. In the second period, capital (machine) is introduced; and productivity improves. The laborer is separated from capital. That is, the capitalist and investors own the tools of production. Laborers are hired to produce the product -- salmon. Capitalists and investors enjoy a surplus value, which attracts more investment and labor into this business, and the production expands. The result is Period Three. As the production expands, more products are put on the market, and prices fall until they reach a new equilibrium: the fourth period.

Row 2. Direct labor on the second row records the amount of average socially necessary labor used in production. Remember that in the **Table 1. 18**

1	Period	1	2	3	4
2	Direct labor (hr)	100	100	500	500
3	Capital (hr)	0	100	500	500
4	Output (Q)	100	300	1500	1500
5	Cost (hr)	1	0.67	0.67	0.67
6	Wages (hr)	100	≤ 100	$455 < w < 500$	460
7	Wages ($)	$100	$\leq \$100$	$\$455 < w < 500$	$460
8	Return to the capitalists (hr)	0	> 100	$545 > p > 500$	500
9	Monetary return on capital ($)	0	$> \$100$	$\$545 > p > 500$	$500
10	Price of salmon ($)	$1	$1 > x > 0.67$	0.67	0.64
11	Salmon per hour	1	1.5	1.5	1.5
12	Total Revenue ($)	$100	$300 > x > 201$	1000	960

first period, the laborers worked for themselves, but from the second period on, the laborers work for the capitalists or investors.

Row 3. The third row is capital recorded in terms of the amount of socially necessary labor needed to produce the capital stock. This value refers to the capital used up, not the total value of the machine. (For example, a machine costs 100 labor hours and it can only produce 200 salmon. If 50 salmon are produced, then the capital used is only 25% the value of the machine, or 25 labor hours are actually used.)

Row 4. The output is the quantity of the product, the number of salmon produced.

Row 5. Cost per product is a way of measuring the productivity in terms of the average socially necessary labor hours needed to produce one salmon. This is calculated by dividing the total output of the product by the total amount of direct (row 2) and indirect labor (row 3) used. Notice that the cost is reduced from Period 1 to Period 2, because productivity improvement machinery has been introduced. There is no price change from Period 2 to Period 4.

Row 6. Wages in terms of labor hours is the compensation to laborers. The number in the second and third periods is a transitory number. In an economy, if an average labor hour produces 10 fish, and the laborer is paid only 5 fish per hour, we say that the laborer is paid only 0.5 labor hours for each labor hour of work.

Row 7. Wages ($) is monetary compensation to the laborer. It is found by converting the compensation listed in row 6 from labor hours to monetary terms. We assume that $1.00 is equivalent to one labor hour. This applies to all 4 periods.

Row 8. Return to the capitalist is measured by the average of the socially necessary labor hours. The numbers in the second and third periods are transitory numbers. At equilibrium, investors get exactly what is invested in terms of average socially necessary labor hours. In other words, the surplus value will be zero.

Row 9. Monetary return on capital is found by converting row 8 from labor hours to monetary terms. ($1.00 is equivalent to one average labor hour.)

Row 10. Price of salmon is obtained by converting the cost per product in labor hour (row 5) to monetary terms. ($1/labor hour × row 5). In Period 2, the price of salmon stays in a range limited by the cost per product (row 5).

Row 11. Salmon per hour is an indicator of productivity. The more salmon produced per labor hour, the higher the productivity is. This is calculated by dividing the output (row 4) by the sum of the direct labor plus capital (rows 2 and 3).

Row 12. Total revenue is the total revenue of the salmon products produced by this one producer, Mr. Fujimoto. It is determined by multiplying the price of salmon (row 10) by the quantity of the product (row 4).

Suppose that in Period 1, 100 hours of direct labor can produce 100 salmon without any capital. Thus, the cost per salmon is 1 labor hour. At equilibrium, goods are exchanged with equal value; therefore, the compensation to the laborer is 100 labor hours, or $100 in monetary terms. The price is $1 per salmon. The productivity is 1 salmon per average labor hour.

Suppose that in Period 2, capital is introduced, in the form of machinery that can improve productivity. For every 100 direct labor hours, 100 labor hours of capital will be used. The output increases to 300 salmon. The equilibrium price of each salmon decreases to 0.67 average labor hours [(100+100)hr /300 salmon = 0.67]. There is a 50% (row 11) productivity improvement for salmon production. For the sake of simplicity, assume there is a 10% productivity improvement in the economy from Periods 1 to 4. Mr. Fujimoto does not have to pay more to his laborers. He can pay the same wages as if they worked for themselves, or he can pay even less, even though laborers want to improve their standard of living. He can do this first because there is an army of unemployed people. Second, as the economy experiences an overall productivity improvement, a price decrease occurs for average goods under the condition that $1 is equivalent to 1 labor hour throughout the 4 periods.

To illustrate this last point, assume that $1 is equivalent to 1 labor hour throughout the 4 periods, and that $100 can purchase 100 average goods. As the productivity of the economy improves 10%, the same $100 will be able to purchase 110 goods. The purchasing power of the same $100 has increased 10%. The bottom line for workers is that they demand a standard of living, or purchasing power of their wages, that is at least the same as before. Since a 10% productivity improvement of the economy results in purchasing power increase by 10% under the condition that $1 is equivalent to one labor hour, the question instead becomes how much money will be needed to purchase 100 goods? It can be calculated as follows:

$$\$100/110 \text{ goods} \times 100 \text{ goods} = \$90.90$$

Mr. Fujimoto must pay the workers at least $90.90 after a 10% productivity improvement in the general economy if he previously paid $100 for the same amount of work.

For the reason stated above, row 6 and row 7 in Period 2 have a number less than 100. Mr. Fujimoto naturally expects his capital investment to bring a profit. This is why rows 8 and 9 are larger than 100, which is the capital used in the production. Notice that the sum of hours of total compensation given to the direct labor and capital is larger than what was put in (see row 12). This could happen because productivity is improving faster than the average rate of productivity improvement of the salmon industry as a whole. In other words, if, on average, it takes 0.95 hours to produce one salmon in the economy, the 300 salmon produced in Period 2 by Mr. Fujimoto will be equivalent to 300 x 0.95 = 285 average socially necessary labor hours. Thus, in Period Two, an input of 200 labor hours produces an output of 285 labor hour if the average time the economy needs to produce one salmon is 0.95 hours (row 5). Notice that it only takes Mr. Fujimoto 0.67 hours to produce one salmon. However, this is a transitory condition; it will not last. Because there is a production increase as more and more money moves into this profitable business, as a result the supply increases at the market. The price of salmon will fall from the original $1 (row 10 Period One). The cost of salmon is 0.67 labor hours (see row 5, Period 2), or $0.67. This means that the price of salmon will not go lower than $0.67, for below this price investors will lose money. If the price moves lower than $0.67, the market mechanism will move the price up by driving some salmon producers out of business. Thus, the price is between $1 and $0.67 per salmon, suggesting that there is plenty of profit to be made by simply increasing production.

A production expansion is illustrated in Period 3. The rate of salmon produced per hour (row 11) has increased from 1 to 1.5 from Period 1 to Period 2. The total revenue is between $300 and $201. To illustrate how much profit can be made, we need to assume a level of revenue, say it is $260 for Period 2, after paying $210 for the cost of capital and labor (you can assume any number larger than or equal to 200, but reasonably close to 200). There is still a $50 surplus value left for Mr. Fujimoto. However, surplus value is transitory.

Period 3 presents an equilibrium point where total revenue represents the total labor input. This was the equilibrium in the previous salmon model. Suppose Mr. Fujimoto expands his production. Direct labor increases from 100 to 500 labor hours, as did the machinery (row 3, Period 3). Total production output increases from 300 to 1500, compared with Period 2. Cost remains the same: 0.67 labor hours. At equilibrium, the price falls back to $0.67 (row 10), equivalent to the labor necessary to produce the goods. At this price level, the total revenue is $1000. Mr. Fujimoto wants more profit for his investment. Therefore, he pays his workers less than $1 per labor hour. The question is, how much lower can Mr. Fujimoto push the wage?

In order to find the lowest wage workers will accept, first we assume the economy has a 10% productivity improvement from Period 1 to Period 3, while the $1 remains equivalent to 1 labor hour. Workers demand that their standard of living does not fall. For a direct labor input of 500 labor hours, what is the minimum wage that Mr. Fujimoto can potentially pay? The lowest wage is that which achieves the same amount of purchasing power in Period 3 as in Period 1.

Suppose that $500 can purchase 500 average goods in Period One. This represents the pay rate in Period 1 (Period 1, row 1 and row 7). As the economy grows with a 10% productivity improvement rate, the $500 can purchase 500 × (1 + 10%) goods under the condition that $1 is equivalent to 1 labor hour.

$$500 \times (1 + 10\%) = 550 \text{ average goods in Period 3}$$

How much money is needed to purchase the 500 average goods in Period 3?

$$\$500/550 \text{ goods} \times 500 \text{ goods} = \$455$$

This is the amount of money Mr. Fujimoto will pay the workers for 500 labor hours of work but only if the workers will accept the same standard of living as in Period 1. As we know from the lobster model, under full employment Mr. Fujimoto will pay no more than 500 hours for the 500 labor hours of work. Thus, we find a range within which an agreement between the laborer and the capitalists can be reached: 454 hours to 500 hours. In monetary terms, it is in $454 to $500 range. What Mr. Fujimoto will actually pay the workers depends on their relative negotiating powers.

Based on the range of compensation that workers will accept, we can find the range of returns on capital in terms of labor hours and in monetary terms, since the total revenue at equilibrium is the same regardless of how workers and capitalists divide the total revenue (row 8, and row 9 in Period 3) (row 9 = row 12 – row 7).

In Period 3, although the total revenue represents an equal

exchange of value, it is not a true equilibrium point, because there is surplus value. Suppose an agreement is made between the laborers and Mr. Fujimoto that Mr. Fujimoto will pay $460 for 500 labor hours. Mr. Fujimoto will have made a $40 surplus value. This will attract more capital into this type of business.

In Period 4, a true equilibrium is presented where surplus value has been driven to zero. Assume that the workers' compensation can be held at the same level as in Period 3, and as more products are produced, the price will fall until the surplus value reaches zero. We assume that Mr. Fujimoto does not expand production, while other businesses expand their production of salmon. At this point, workers are paid $460 for their 500 labor hours of work, and Mr. Fujimoto gets $500 for his capital investment. The total revenue decreases from $1000 in Period 3 to $960 ($460 + $500) in Period 4. Thus, the total salmon output stays the same as 1500. The price of the salmon must be:

$$\$960/1500 = \$0.64$$

This is shown on row 10, Period 4.

If the price per salmon becomes $0.64, then the input of 1000 labor hours in Period 4 is only equivalent to $960 (row 12). Does this appear to contradict the assumption that $1 is equivalent to 1 labor hour? No, because the $1 as equivalent to 1 labor hour is the average figure for the whole economy. While there is some deviation at equilibrium for the salmon industry, it does not change the overall figure, as the salmon industry represents only a small fraction of the economy. Changes in other industries in the economy may offset this deviation.

CONCLUSION OF MARKET MODEL 12

In a competitive market, under less than full employment, when capital investment produces a productivity improvement):

1.   At the equilibrium point, surplus value is zero. Surplus value exists as a transitory phenomenon.

2.   Labor will get short-changed. The exchange between labor and capital no longer complies to the equal exchange of value. The negotiation power of labor and capital determines the compensation of labor.

3.   In most cases, laborers enjoy only a fraction of the fruits of

productivity improvement. For example, if there is a 10% productivity improvement in the economy, the laborers will most likely enjoy an standard of living increase between 0% and 10%.

4.   The price of the goods in this particular industry will fall as a result of the decreasing compensation to labor relative to its value. The price of a good will fall below the labor value of the commodity.

MARKET MODEL 13 (WITHOUT DEFLATION, WITHOUT FULL EMPLOYMENT, SEPARATION OF LABORERS AND CAPITAL)

There is deflation in the above salmon model. This model is to study what happens when there is no deflation? Or inflation = 0. We will use Model 12, only making necessary changes so that the inflation rate is zero.

The average productivity improvement rate of the economy in the concerned Period 1 to Period 4 is 10%. From this we know the previous assumption that $1 = 1 labor hour for all four periods will have to change. Assume in Period 1, the ratio is ($1 = 1 labor hour). It will become $1.10 = 1 labor hour in Period 4. This reason was explained in Model 11 by using Table 1.16.

This model (Table 1.19) represents constant price, without full employment. Model 12 (the salmon model) is reproduced here with minor changes. We only need to examine Period 1 and Period 4; therefore, Period 2 and 3 have been deleted. The factor 1.10 has been used to multiply any row with a dollar sign in Period 4 of the original table to get this new Period 4 dollar amount in Table 1.19.

All conditions remain the same as in the previous model, except that the price level has zero inflation. Notice that the total monetary revenue in Period 4 becomes $1056, up from $960 in the previous deflation model. The price of salmon in Period 4 becomes $0.70 a piece, up from $0.64 in the previous deflation model. Wages ($) to laborers increase to $506, from $460 in the previous deflation model. Return on capital becomes $550, up from $500 in the previous model.

Table 1. 19

1	Period	1	4
2	Direct labor (hr)	100	500
3	Capital (hr)	0	500
4	Output (Q)	100	1500
5	Cost (hr)	1	0.67
6	Wages (hr)	100	460
7	Wages ($)	$100	$506
8	Return to the capitalists (hr)	0	500
9	Monetary return on capital ($)	0	$550
10	Price of salmon ($)	$1	$0.70
11	Salmon per hour	1	1.5
12	Total Revenue ($)	$100	$1056

CONCLUSION OF MARKET MODEL 13

From Table 1.19, we can make the following conclusions: (Under a perfect competitive market, with zero inflation, without full employment, at equilibrium)(I = 0):

1.   The monetary compensation to laborers increases at a rate less than the average productivity improvement rate of the economy (L $\leq$ S).

2.   The monetary return on capital increases at a rate equal to the average productivity improvement rate of the economy (P = S).

3.   The price of goods will fall if production improves at a better rate than that of the economy in general.

4.   There is no surplus value at equilibrium.

5.   At equilibrium, capital is exchanged according to the rule of equal exchange of value, but labor is not.

EXAMPLE OF APPLICATIONS

What happens to an industry that does not show any productivity improvements? There are two cases to consider: the first is a competitive market with full employment; the second is a competitive market without full employment. In the first case, the equilibrium of exchange always occurs at equal exchange of value. In the second case, however, the equilibrium of exchange does not always happen at the equal exchange of value, especially when labor is involved.

APPLICATION CASE ONE (with full employment)

Suppose an economy is experiencing a 10% productivity growth per year with inflation equal to zero. Suppose the education industry has not made any improvements in productivity. From the analysis of the previous model, we know that there is a 10% increase in the monetary value for one labor hour. If one labor hour at the beginning of the year is equivalent to $20, the one labor hour at the end of the year will be equivalent to $22. [$20 × (1 + 10%)]. Suppose one year of higher education at a university costs 1000 labor hours. At the beginning of the year, the university will charge $20 x 1000 labor hours = $20,000 tuition. That is what the students need to pay for one year of higher education if the students pay at the start of the year. At the end of the year, the university will need to charge $22 x 1000 labor hours = $22,000 tuition. We obtain this by applying the rule of equal exchange of value at equilibrium.

APPLICATION CASE TWO (without full employment)

Suppose an economy is experiencing 10% productivity growth a year with inflation equal to zero. Suppose, again, that the education industry has not made any productivity improvements. If one labor hour at the beginning of the year is, on average, equivalent to $20, the one labor hour at the end of the year will be equivalent to $22 due to the 10% increase in monetary value of one labor hour. Suppose one year of higher education costs 1000 labor hour. At the beginning of the year, the university will charge $20 x 1000 labor hours = $20,000 tuition. At the end of the year, the university will need to charge $22 x 1000 labor hours = $22,000 tuition, if the equilibrium is at equal exchange of value. Similar to the salmon model without full employment, the price of the product, in this case tuition, will be lower than $22,000. The equilibrium tuition is somewhere between $20,000 and $22,000.

SUMMARY OF APPLICATION

In summary, for an industry that does not have any productivity changes over a range of time, the price of the product or service will increase. In a perfect competitive market with full employment and zero inflation, the price increase rate will be equal to the productivity improvement rate of the economy. In a perfect competitive market without full employment and with zero inflation, the price increase rate will be larger than zero, but less than the productivity improvement rate of the economy.

NOTES ON THE CONCEPT

The central idea of this chapter is that the equilibrium point of exchange is determined by the "labor value" necessary to reproduce the goods. This is true because, in most cases, goods are exchanged by the rule of equal exchange of value. The phrase "labor value" in the above sentence refers to labor embedded in the goods that is required to reproduce the goods by current means of production, not by the labor needed to produce it under past means of production. For example, a digital watch, when first introduced, was sold for $3000. Today, it costs only about $20. In terms of labor, a watch, when first introduced, may have cost an average of 100 labor hours. Today it might cost only a fraction of that. (All figures are hypothetical.)

However, we should notice that even when surplus value becomes zero at equilibrium, workers are still short-changed when there is no full employment. Surplus value is a transitory phenomenon.

SUMMARY OF CONCLUSIONS

1. The methodology of this work is different from that of mainstream economics. The market economic system is basically sound, but an economic policy remedy is necessary to fix the defects of the system. Economists should not only ask how the market economy works, but also how it should work. Economic theory should be tested by reality.

2. The subject of this study is the market economy. The theory developed in this book is applicable to any market economy, regardless of the ideology of the government of that particular economy.

3. The purpose of economics is to achieve the most efficient means of resource allocation through understanding the inner workings of the market economy. By making a market economic system work efficiently, we can improve the material well-being of human life.

4. Economic efficiency is defined as desirable material output per average human labor hour input. The basic, essential, and, indeed, only economic resource for the purpose of a study of economic efficiency is human labor.

5. The economic efficiency of a market economy is related to how the prices of goods are determined and how they should be determined. Because of the difficulty in studying price movement, we instead study the average price movement. The average realized price is the value or exchange value of goods.

6. Karl Marx and Adam Smith, among others, developed the labor theories of value. Their theories face challenges from different schools of economic thought. A collection of these challenges is summarized in the list of paradoxes.

7. Commodities have two characteristics, use value and exchange value. Goods that have exchange value must also have use value. Goods that have use value may not have exchange value.

8. Price movement is centered around the socially average labor hour required to produce the goods. A natural force moves price toward labor value. At equilibrium, price correctly reflects the labor value.

9.   The law of perfect markets: equal exchange value is the rule for perfect markets. The value of a commodity is determined by the socially necessary labor to reproduce it. When two goods change hands at equilibrium, they exchange with equal value. Since both the buyer and seller want the best and most profitable exchange, they will only agree to exchange goods at the point where the buyer's payment and seller's goods have the same value. When goods are exchanged according to the law of equal exchange of value, economic resources can be optimally allocated.

Under perfect competitive market conditions, at equilibrium, the exchange happens at an equal exchange of value.

10.   The following are conditions for a perfect competitive market:
*   People at markets are motivated by their own material interest. They want to gain as much as possible in the exchange of goods at the market.
*   Each participant can switch to and from one trade to another. There is no restriction in switching between producing different goods.
*   The producer can decide what to produce, when to produce, where to produce, how to produce, and what quality to produce. There is also free entry to production, free flow of factors of production, and free flow of factors of consumption.
*   Each producer has information on other producers. No single producer can control the price. There are many producers for each product.

11.   In a perfect competitive market with full employment and zero inflation, we discover:

            A.   The monetary compensation to labor increases at a rate equal to the social productivity improvement rate of the economy.

            B.   The monetary return on capital also increases at a rate equal to the social productivity improvement rate of the economy.

            C.   The price of goods will fall if the production improves more quickly than that of the general economy.

            D.   There is no surplus value at equilibrium.

            E.   Wages and capital are exchanged according to

the rule of equal exchange of value at equilibrium.

12. In a competitive market with deflation and less than full employment, when capital investment produces a productivity improvement, we have the following conclusions:

- At equilibrium, surplus value is zero. Surplus exists as a transitory phenomenon.

- Laborers get short-changed. The exchange between laborer and capitalist no longer conforms to the law of equal exchange of value. The negotiation power of laborer and capitalist determines the mount of compensation to laborer.

- In most cases, laborers enjoy only a fraction of the fruit of productivity improvement. For example, if there is a 10% productivity improvement in an economy, the workers most likely enjoy an increase in standard of living between 0% and 10%.

- The price of goods in this particular industry will fall as a result of decreasing compensation to laborers, relative to the value. The price of a good will fall below the labor value of the commodity.

13. Under a perfect competitive market, with zero inflation, without full employment, we discover at equilibrium:

- The monetary compensation to the labor increases at a rate less than the average social productivity improvement rate of the economy.

- The monetary return to the capitalist increases at a rate equal to the average social productivity improvement rate of the economy.

- The price of goods will fall if the production of the goods enjoys a better than average productivity improvement rate of the economy.

- There is no surplus value at equilibrium.

- At equilibrium, capital is exchanged by the rule of equal exchange of value, while labor is not.

14. Under perfect market conditions, at equilibrium, when the producer enjoys the same productivity improvement rate as the average productivity improvement rate of the economy and when the price of the goods concerned increases at the same speed as the inflation rate of the economy, we have the following relations:

$$(1 + L) = (1 + P) = (1 + R) = (1 + S)(1 + I)$$

Where:

L: labor compensation increase rate

P: profit rate of the producer

R: interest rate

S: productivity improvement rate of either producer or economy

I: inflation rate

15.   For the industry that does not make any productivity changes over time, the price of the product or service will increase. In a perfect competitive market with full employment and zero inflation, the price increase rate will be equal to the rate of productivity improvement of the economy. In a perfect competitive market without full employment and with zero inflation, the price increase rate of the particular good will be larger than zero, but less than the productivity improvement rate of the general economy.

CHAPTER 2

OPTIMAL ECONOMIC PARAMETERS FOR IDEAL ECONOMY

INTRODUCTION

This chapter will try to answer the following several questions. What will it be like if we maximize the efficiency of a market economy based on the theory of labor value. If we maximize the efficiency of the market economy based on the theory of labor value, would there be any profit for business? Is there still interest on loans? What kind of relationship is there between profit and economic efficiency? What is the relationship between interest rate and economic efficiency? What is the relationship between labor cost and economic efficiency?

To answer all the above questions, we need to go through a series of thought experiments. First, we need to define a virtual economy, which is not a real economy. It is not the U.S. economy; it is not the Japanese economy; and it is not any particular economy in existence. Next, we will study what happens if we try to maximize the efficiency of this virtual economy.

THE VIRTUAL ECONOMY

The virtual economy is a market economy with common characteristics of all real market economies. The virtual economy is an abstract model of the real world market economy. The virtual economy does not refer to a specific market, such as the U.S. market economy, the China market economy, and the Germany market economy. The virtual economy is the theoretical image of a market economic system. In this virtual economy, there are key elements of the market economy, such as consumers, producers, prices of goods, wages rate, inflation rate, interest rates and profit. The following will examine how the efficiency of the market system can be optimized, and maximized.

MAXIMIZE SATISFACTION TO MEET HUMAN NEEDS AND WANTS

The purpose of human economic activity is to satisfy human needs and wants for goods and services. Therefore, the efficiency of the economic system can be measured by how well it serves those needs and wants. For this reason, when measure the efficiency of the market economy, I will compare the output (the goods and services consumed), to the input (human labor). The human labor, as presented in the earlier chapter, is the current labor value embedded into goods and services. It is the socially necessary labor hours used during the processes of producing and delivering the goods and services to consumers.

The ultimate purpose of all human economic activity is to meet the needs and desires of human consumption. A need could be clean air, or a clean ocean, or even the desire to keep endangered species alive. It is only natural that the study of economic efficiency should start at how to maximize satisfaction to human needs and wants. Consumption in a market economy consists of two parts, private consumption and public consumption. Public consumption refers to the consumption facilitated by government purchasing power. All non-government consumption is referred to as private consumption. We will start our analysis with private consumption. Public consumption has the same characteristics as private consumption. Therefore, the following analysis for private consumption can also apply to the public consumption.

MAXIMIZE EFFICIENCY OF CONSUMPTION

This section presents a single good consumption case and introduces the concept of diminishing marginal utility.

In a market economy, consumers purchase goods to satisfy their needs and wants. For instance, Mr. Chen buys a bottle of soda because he is thirsty. Ms. Lin purchases an apple to eat since the apple satisfies her desire for a fruit. For goods to have a value so that customers will pay a price to purchase them, the goods must be useful to the buyer. Consumers will pay for goods or services only if they cannot get them for free. The objective of an economy is to maximize the satisfaction of consumers by providing them with goods and services. Therefore, we start by examining how to maximize the satisfaction of a consumer. Next, I will discover the relationship between maximization of satisfaction and the value of labor.

DIMINISHING MARGINAL UTILITY

To understand how goods satisfy consumers, we need to have a measurement for the satisfaction. This measurement is called utility. Utility is a measurement of how much a particular item of goods can satisfy a consumer. The higher the level of utility, the more it can satisfy a consumer. The utility of goods has a tendency to drop. For example, to a consumer the utility of eating an apple changes as more apples get into the stomach (Table 2.1). To illustrate, economists have discovered the following utility patterns on consumer consumption. For the first apple, the consumer has a utility level of 4, the second apple has 3.5, the third has 2, the forth apple has 0, and the fifth apple has negative 2 utility. The consumer gets 4 utility for the first apple, 3.5 utility for the second apple, 2 utility for the third, and so on.

Table 2. 1

Apples Consumed	Marginal Utility
1	4
2	3.5
3	2
4	0
5	-2

The more the consumer eats, the less utility he gains for each additional apple. This is called the diminishing marginal utility on consumption. The number given for each utility level indicates the relative usefulness and satisfaction of the goods or services to a consumer. The number is a relative measurement in relation to other levels of utility.

The number is not absolute. For example, we cannot compare the marginal utility level generated by the first apple for two different persons. If Adam claims his first apple of the day gives him pleasure at level 5, and Susan claims her first apple of the day gives her pleasure at level 1000, we could not, however, tell who has more pleasure and satisfaction with the first apple. The utility level is relative only to a particular person.

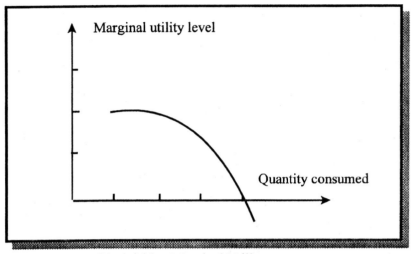

Figure 2.1   Diminishing Marginal Utility

The diminishing marginal utility (Figure 2.1) presents the fact that the utility of goods to a consumer decreases, as each additional sample of the goods is consumed. The utility can become negative if too much is consumed. To maximize the total utility for a consumer, the consumer must keep consuming until the marginal utility reaches zero. However, this assumes that the consumer can afford all the merchandise or services. In reality, the situation is different. Since no one can afford unlimited vocations, an unlimited number of houses, an unlimited number of automobiles, an unlimited number of boats, unlimited amounts of entertainment, or an unlimited number of airplanes. Therefore, it is necessary to introduce consumption constraints when we study the maximization of utility. For any given utility curve that has diminishing marginal utility, the increase in total utility necessarily results in a decrease in marginal utility. As more of the goods are consumed, the increase in the quantity of the consumption moves the consumption point on the utility curve to the right, where the marginal utility is lower. In other words, the decrease in marginal utility could necessarily mean an increase in total utility, as long as the marginal utility is positive.

UTILITY MAXIMIZATION FOR TWO GOODS

Next we will discuss a two goods case. Here is the list of assumptions we will use in the following two merchandise discussions.

1.   There are only two goods. The consumer can consume one type of good or the other type of good or both.
2.   The consumer earns his own income. He is an average laborer. According to the labor theory of value, if he works two hours, he will make a two labor hour value contribution to the product. We assume there is no taxation.
3.   We ignore the effect of time. The utility a person has changes from year to year; last year the consumer may have preferred apples to pears, while this year he may like pears better than apples. To avoid this variation, we will study the utility maximization for a particular moment. At this moment, we assume the consumer has a constant utility preference for goods.
4.   Instead of using any currency unit, we use labor value to directly measure the price of the goods. This is no different from using a currency unit, since the difference between the two is only a ratio. For example, one labor hour value may be worth $15.

In a two goods case, we will study how consumers maximize utility. Assume a consumer has money in the amount of 5 labor hours. Since he is an average laborer, it will take him 5 labor hours of work to earn it. We assume there is no taxation. There are two goods: fish and pork. The fish costs 1 labor hour per kilogram, while the pork costs 2 labor hours per kilogram. The utility Table 2.2 shows how much utility will be produced from each additional kilogram of fish and pork.

Next let us discuss how the consumer will decide which and how many to consume (Table 2.2). To simplify the thought process, we assume the fish or pork can only be consumed one kilogram at a time. This means there is no consumption of half of a kilogram, or a fraction of a kilogram, of pork or fish. Bear in mind that we have limited resources in this case. The limitation is the 5 hours of labor value. To maximize the total utility, we should maximize the marginal utility for each additional labor hour we spend. To start with, if the consumer eats 1 kilogram of pork, he will have a satisfaction level of 5 utility, this will cost him 2 labor hours. The marginal utility per labor hour for taking pork is 2.5 (5 utility/2 labor hours). The fish only costs 1 labor hour per kilogram. Therefore, the marginal utility per labor hour for the fish is 4 (4 utility/1 labor hour). So the consumer eats the one kilogram of fish and compares the marginal utility again. This time the fish still has the highest utility level, so he eats fish again for the second kilogram. His marginal utility for the second kilogram of fish is 3. When he compares the marginal utility again, the pork becomes more attractive, so he eats a kilogram of pork, which has the marginal utility of 2.5. By now, he has consumed 2 kilograms of fish and 1 kilogram of pork. When comparing the marginal utility this time, he finds the fish is more attractive. He eats another kilogram of fish. At the end, he has used up all his purchasing power. He ate 3 kilograms of fish and 1 kilogram of pork. This story depicts the process of utility maximization by means of comparing

Table 2. 2

Quantity Consumed	Fish Utility	Pork Utility
1	4	5
2	3	3
3	1.5	1
4	0	-1

marginal utility per labor hour. When we talk about marginal utility, we must distinguish between two types of marginal utility. Marginal utility can mean the utility produced by the last unit of goods. It can also mean the utility produced by an additional labor hour. When we maximize total utility, we compare the marginal utility per additional labor hour for the goods and use the one that provides the maximum marginal utility per additional labor hour. When goods are infinitely dividable, total utility will be maximized when the marginal utility of additional labor hours over all goods are equalized.

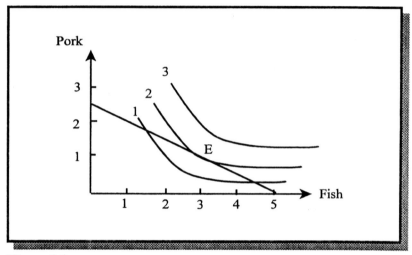

Figure 2.2

In Figure 2.2, the straight line connecting the vertical axis and the horizontal axis is the production possibility curve. Every point on that line defines two goods in their maximum amount that the consumer can produce. Given the 5 labor hours, and that the cost of producing fish and pork is 1 labor hour and 2 labor hours respectively, we can calculate how much fish the consumer can produce if he uses all the labor hours to produce fish.

This is:

5 labor hours /1 labor hour = 5 kilograms of fish

Likewise, we can calculate how much pork he can produce if he uses all the labor hours to produce pork.

This is:

5 labor hours/2 labor hours = 2.5 kilograms of pork

The point (0, 2.5) is on the vertical axis at 2.5 kilograms of pork. The point (5,0) is the point on the horizontal axis that represents 5 kilograms of fish. The connection of these two points forms the production possibility curve. In this case, the production possibility curve is a straight line, even though in some other cases it could be a concaved curve. Every point at the left side of the curve and every point on the production possibility curve represents the possible combination of products that can be produced within a given input restriction of 5 labor hours. Every point at the right side of the straight line is impossible to produce given the restriction of 5 labor hours in this case. The convex curve that meets with the straight line is the utility indifference curve. Every point on this utility indifference curve represents the same utility level for the consumer. For any two randomly picked points on the utility indifference curve, a consumer has no preference for one over the other. There are three utility indifference curves on Figure 2.2. They are labeled 1, 2, and 3. The Number 1 has a lower utility level than that of Number 2. The Number 2 has a lower utility level than that of Number 3. Although Number 3 has the highest utility level, it is at the right side of the production possibility curve; thus it is not possible to achieve within the given production possibility curve. The maximum point of utility maximization is reached at point E, where the Number 2 curve meets with the production possibility curve. The production possibility curve is also called a consumption possibility curve, or purchasing possibility curve, since it defines the limit for consumption and purchasing possibility.

What is discussed above can also be put into mathematical formula.

Total Utility =   utility of fish (quantity of fish) + utility of pork (quantity of pork)

Quantity of fish = labor hours used for fish /cost of fish
Quantity of pork = labor hours used for pork /cost of pork

Constraint:

5 labor hours = labor hours used for fish + labor hours used for pork

UTILITY MAXIMIZATION FOR "N" GOODS

In an "n" goods case, maximization of utility requires the marginal utility per labor hour equal over all the different products, with a given constraint. The following formula presents the "n" goods case where a consumer with limited purchasing power faces the choice of "n" goods or services. The symbol "n" could be any integer. The formula presents how the utility is maximized. The total utility will be maximized if the consumer will always consume the products or services that bear the highest marginal utility for each additional cost. The cost refers to the price of goods. It can be presented in the unit of labor hours.

"N" Goods Case:

Total Utility = utility 1 (goods 1(x1)) + utility 2(goods 2(x2)) + utility 3(goods3 (x3))+ ......

Constraint:
x labor hours = sum of (x1, x2, x3, ...)

Where:
Utility 1 represents the utility produced by the consumption of good 1. Similarly for utility 2, utility 3, so on. "good 1" is the quantity of good 1 consumed, similarly for good 2, good 3 and so on.

x1, x2, x3, are the labor hours used in particular good consumption, x1 is the amount of labor value used in the consumption of good 1; x2 is the amount of labor value used in the consumption of good 2, so on. "x" is the total labor hours the consumer has.

Mathematically, to maximize the total utility in the above equation, we can take the derivative and solve the functions for the maximum utility. You will find that, as consumers maximize utility, the marginal utility per cost will be equalized over all goods available to the consumer for a given expenditure constraint when the goods are infinitely dividable.

CRITICS OF SUBJECTIVE VALUE THEORY

There are many opponents of the labor theory of value. One important opposing theory is the marginalist theory of value. There are a number of theoretical problems with subjective value theory. The marginalist claims the value of goods is determined not by the labor needed to produce it or reproduce it, instead it is determined by the marginal utility it generates for the consumer.

1.   In the first experiment, suppose we give Susan $10 for grocery shopping. Susan buys the following goods: one kilogram of vegetables, one bottle of milk, and one loaf of bread. In the second experiment, suppose we give $50 to Susan for grocery shopping instead of $10. With $50, she buys two kilograms of vegetables, two bottles of milk, and three loaves of bread, and many other things. For simplicity, we assume the price of goods did not change during our two shopping experiments. The two shopping experiments are so similar in time and space that Susan's utility indifference curve has not changed. As we know, marginal utility is diminishing as more and more goods are purchased and consumed. So the marginal utility for three loaves of bread is lower than the marginal utility of one loaf of bread. Thus the value of the bread is lower in the second experiment than in the first experiment. That is to say, the price of bread in the second experiment should be lower than that in the first experiment. Similarly, according to the marginal value theory, the price of vegetables and milk should also be cheaper than those items in the first experiment. Why is the price not actually affected by any single shopper's change in the quantity of goods purchased? Or consumed?

2.   Some economists argue that the price of a good is determined by the total utility of the good. For instance, the price of apple is determined by the total utility level generated by the consumption of the apples by a consumer. As in the above, suppose Susan just bought the following goods: apples, pears, oranges, vegetables, milk, and bread. We may want to ask her which one produces the most utility or satisfaction for her, and she may answer "the bread." We may go to check the price of

the bread and discover that in most cases it is not the most expensive thing she just purchased. If the utilitarianism value theory is right, the price of goods is determined by the total utility of a good. The bread will be the most expensive of all Susan's goods. We may want to observe what people purchase at stores, and ask them which one creates the most utility for them, then go back to check the price of the goods. I am sure we will not be surprised how often the utilitarianism value of theory is wrong.

3.   The price of personal computers has been falling since the personal computer was invented. If the utility or marginal utility of a product determines its price, we can safely infer that the utility or marginal utility of computers is falling fast. The facts point to the contrary. The utility of the personal computer is increasing over the years, as the personal computer becomes more powerful and software becomes more user-friendly with more powerful functions. The marginal utility and total utility measure the consumers' subjective views on the computer. Do consumers' subjective views determine the continuing fall of the price of the personal computer? Of course not. Does productivity improvement play any role at all in determinating the price of a computer?

4.   Marginalists believe the exchange value is determined by marginal utility of both trading parties. Each trading party maximizes his or her utility, pleasure, or satisfaction. The higher the marginal utility, the higher the exchange value. So industrial goods that have little or no use to the producer, should have little or no exchange value. One evidence for the lack of marginal utility for industrial goods is that the producer does not want to keep any of them for himself. Every thing he produced is to be used for exchange of other goods, namely money. Therefore, according to the marginalist theory, the exchange value of industrial goods must be extremely low. Contrary to marginalist theory, many industrial goods are extremely expensive. A jumbo commercial aircraft, for example, is extremely expensive.

5.   According to mainstream economics, marginal utility is equal to price. That is:

MU = P
Where:

    MU: marginal Utility
    P: price

However, this does not prove that marginal utility determines the price, or exchange value. There is no causal relationship between the marginal utility and the price. The marginal utility does not cause the price, nor does it determine the price. For example, a man is attracted to a pretty girl. Say the level of attraction is denoted by A, and the level of her beauty is B. Say we have an equation:

    A = B

The higher the level of her beauty, the more the man is attracted to her. We cannot, however, from this conclude that A determines B. How much the man is attracted to the pretty girl is the result, not the cause, of the event. We cannot say that her prettiness is caused by a man's very high level of attraction to her beauty. Her beauty most likely is inherited from her parents, and it is not from the man's appreciation for her beauty. Similarly, marginal utility does not determine the marginal cost, that is, the price.

Let's examine Figure 2.3. The vertical axis is the marginal utility level. It is measured in dollar amounts. The horizontal axis is the quantity of peaches purchased and consumed. There are three utility curves. They are U1, U2, and U3. They represent the utility curves of Adam, Baylor, and Carter respectively. Their utility curves decrease as the quantity consumed increases. When the price of peach is at P1, it did not intersect with any utility curve; therefore, no peaches were consumed. Therefore, peaches do not even have a marginal utility. The price exists before any marginal utility can determine it, thus the marginal utility does not determine the price. When the price is reduced to P2, Adam will consume Q1, Baylor will consume Q2, and Carter will consume zero quantity. Carter's marginal utility still cannot equal any price. In a competitive market, the individual consumer does not have the power to influence the price; therefore, the price is flat. The price level determines where it intersects with the marginal

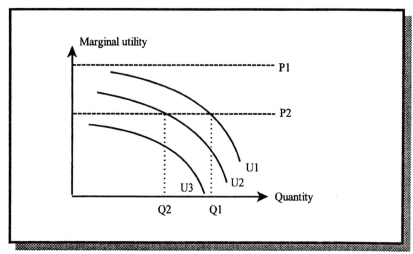

Figure 2.3

utility curve, and where marginal utility will equal the price, not the other way around. The price level of a commodity is determined instead by its labor value needed to reproduce the commodity. The labor value used in the production of the commodity is determined by the productivity of the commodity. Therefore, the marginal utility does not determine the price, or the value of the commodity.

The exchange value theory that serves as the foundation of mainstream economics is that marginal utility is equal to price. A detailed discussion on this is available in the fourth chapter, where we will see why marginal utility does not equal price, which will lead us to examine why the foundation of mainstream economics is wrong.

THE PRICE OF GOODS MUST CORRECTLY REFLECT THE VALUE OF THE GOODS

If we think of a single consumer in a market economy, it does not appear that the price of goods has to reflect the labor value of goods.

The labor value of the goods does not seem to have any relationship with the maximization of any single consumer's utility. For example, Li has $100. He goes to the store and purchases many different goods to maximize his utility. He will maximize his utility for any given pricing structure of the goods regardless of the fact that the price of the goods may not reflect the value of the goods. If the price of apples at $1 per kilogram is the correct price, that reflects the labor hours contained in the apple. It does not seem to matter if the apples sold at $5 per kilogram. The consumer will always maximize his utility with a given amount of purchasing power.

However, if we enlarge our view to include the whole economic process that produces and brings the products to consumers, we will find the maximum of consumer utility and economic efficiency of a market economy can be achieved only if the prices of the goods reflect the values of the goods.

In the above models, we considered the one merchandise case and the two merchandise case. One of the major assumptions is that there is only a single consumer who is also a producer. The only major difference in the above two models is that we increase the number of merchandise from one to two. From the above two models, we understand that the essence of maximizing utility is in maximizing the utility for every unit of labor input that is needed to produce the goods, which are consumed by the same person who produces the goods. The key here is to maximize the utility per labor hour.

To understand the relationship between the utility maximization and the need to have the equilibrium prices of goods reflect the values of the goods, we will introduce some simple tools.

PRODUCTION POSSIBILITY CURVE

Figure 2.4 shows the production possibility curve. Production possibility curves reveal the possible maximum production combination of two products given a fixed level of resources, in our case the given amount of labor hours.

Figure 2.4 illustrates the production possibility curve for Hoover. For a given 8 hours of time, he can produce either 4 kilograms

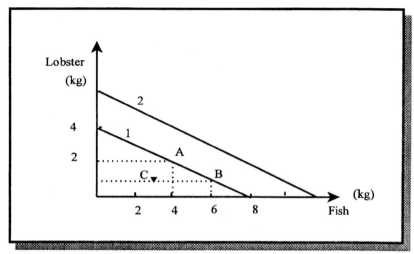

Figure 2.4   Production Possibility Curve

of lobster or 8 kilograms of fish. The curve indicates all possible combinations of output Hoover can produce. Hoover can produce 2 kilograms of lobster and 4 kilograms of fish. This is point A. If he wants to have more fish, he moves down the curve; he can produce 6 kilograms of fish and 1 kilogram of lobster. This is point B.

When the given resources increase or decrease, the production possibility curve shifts. When there are more resources available, the curve shifts to the right, such as with line 2 in Figure 2.4. When there is less economic resource available, the curve shifts to the left. For simplicity, we use a straight line here; the production possibility curve could be a bow-shaped curve. Every point on the curve represents the maximum output of two products with limited input. The area defined by the production possibility curve (the triangular area covered by the curve, the vertical axis, and the horizontal axis), is also possible product combinations for the given limited input. For example, Hoover can produce 2 kilograms of lobster and 4 kilograms of fish given 8 hours time. However, within the given 8 hour time limit, Hoover can produce 1 kilogram of lobster and 3 kilograms of fish. This is presented by point C. This production combination falls in the triangle area defined by the production possibility curve, vertical axis, and horizontal axis.

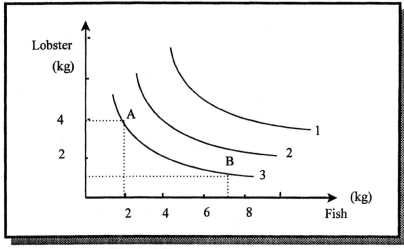

Figure 2.5   Utility Indifference Curve

UTILITY INDIFFERENCE CURVE

Figure 2.5 illustrates the indifference curve. The indifference curve is a convex curve. The points on the curve represent the combination of goods or services that will produce the same satisfaction and pleasure in an individual consumer, in other words, equally preferred by the individual. Figure 2.5 shows three curves for an individual for a particular time period. Say it is one week. There are only three utility indifference curves shown in Figure 2.5, but conceptually there are unlimited indifference curves for a consumer. Although there are only three utility indifference curves shown in Figure 2.5, a consumer actually can have unlimited number of utility indifference curves. Curve 1 has a higher utility level than curve 2; curve 2 has a higher utility level than curve 3. The consumer has equal preference on the same curve. Take curve 3, the individual equally prefers point A or B on the curve. At point A, the individual consumes 4

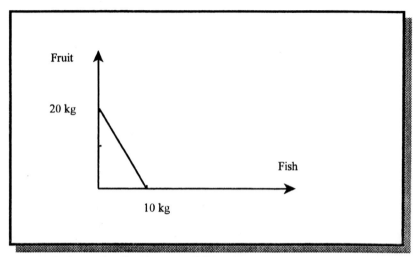

Fruit

20 kg

Fish

10 kg

Figure 2.6   Production Possibility Curve

kg of lobster with 2 kg of fish. At point B, the individual will consume 1 kg of lobster with 7 kg of fish.

PRODUCTION POSSIBILITY CURVE

Suppose we have an individual, who will produce fruit and fish. Let's call him James. For a given 40 hour work week, he will be able to produce 20 kg of fruit. If he uses the 40 hours of work to produce fish, he will get 10 kg of fish. Figure 2.6 shows his production possibility curve. Suppose in his world, $1 is equivalent to one labor hour. So, the 20 kg of fruit is worth $40. The price of the fruit is $2 per kg ($40/20kg). Similarly, the 10 kg of fish is worth of $40. The price of fish is $4 per kg ($40/10kg).

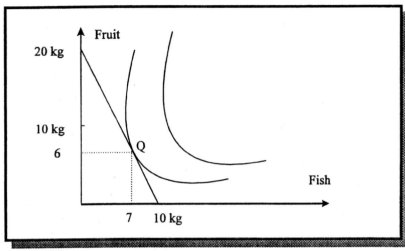

Figure 2.7   Combined Curve

INDIVIDUAL UTILITY MODEL

We also assume James has $40 to spend. From the price of the goods, we can calculate the purchasing possibility curve. See Figure 2.7. It is the same as the production possibility curve, except that the purchasing possibility curve represents the maximum amount of goods this consumer can purchase with a given budget. The price of fruit is $2 per kg. For $40.00, James can purchase 20 kg of fruit. The price of fish is $4.00 per kg. James will be able to purchase 10 kg of fish. We can illustrate James indifference curve and his purchasing possibility curve on Figure 2.7. At point Q, James reaches the maximum utility. At this point, he will consume 6 kg of fruit and 7 kg of fish for the week.When we compare the production possibility curve in Figure 2.6 and the purchasing possibility curve in Figure 2.7, we find the purchasing possibility curve coincides with the production possibility curve. As a result the maximum utility is at point Q. If the production possibility curve is at the left of the purchasing possibility curve, the maximum utility will be restricted to a lower level by the production possibility curve.

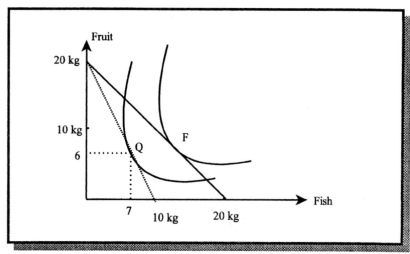

Figure 2.8   Cheap Fish

THE CASE OF CHEAP FISH

In the above case, the price of the goods reflects the labor value. What we want to find out is what will happen if the price of goods does not reflect the labor value. Suppose the price of fish changes, instead of $4.00 per kg of fish, it becomes $2.00 per kg of fish. Figure 2.8 illustrates this situation. Because the price of fish is now $2.00 per kg, James will be able to purchase 20 kg of fish if he decides to use all of his $40.00. The purchasing possibility curve starts at 20 kg of fish on the horizontal axis. The new purchasing possibility curve indicates James can get a higher utility level at point F where his indifference curve is tangent to the purchasing curve. As noted earlier, any point right of the production possibility curve is not achievable with the given economic resources. Point F is at the right side of the production possibility curve; therefore, it is not possible to produce goods at a combination of quantity indicated by point F on Figure 2.8. If James goes ahead and gets the quantity of fish defined by point F, he will not be able to get the quantity of fruit defined by point F. The result is a lower total utility level for James. If James gets the quantity of fruit defined by point F, he will not be able to get the quantity of fish defined by point F. The net result is the same. It has a lower level of utility. In other words, it reduces the total utility for James. James will have less pleasure and satisfaction when the prices of goods do not correctly reflect the value of the goods.

THE CASE OF EXPENSIVE FISH

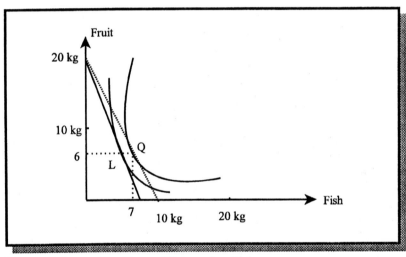

Figure 2.9   The Case of Expensive Fish

If the price of fish becomes more expensive than the price that accurately reflects the labor value of the fish, a different situation may occur. Suppose the price of fish is $5.00 per kg. When James uses all of his $40 to purchase fish, he will be able to purchase 40/5 = 8 kg of fish. The purchasing possibility curve will start on the horizontal axis at 8 kg of fish. Figure 2.9 illustrates the new purchasing possibility curve in a solid line between the two axes. The dotted line represents the production possibility curve, which is also the old purchasing possibility curve when the prices reflect the value of the goods. Point L is the maximum utility level James can get on the new purchasing possibility curve. Point L represents a lower level utility than that of point Q.

CONCLUSION OF INDIVIDUAL MODEL

From the James model, we can conclude that the price of goods must correctly reflect the labor value of the goods for the consumer to achieve the maximum utility and satisfaction.

MAXIMIZATION OF TOTAL UTILITY OF AN ECONOMY

In a modern market economy, there are millions of producers and millions of consumers. In today's large market economy, most commodities are no longer produced by a production unit in the form of a family or a single laborer. The transformation of production from the family and individual base production unit to the corporation (by way of division of labor) also changes the measurement of labor input that is used in the production process from just "labor hour" to "socially necessary labor hour." When we apply the same principle of utility maximization to the market economy where production has become a social event, and in which the process of producing and delivering goods to the consumers has become a collective effort in a society, we will discover that the essence of maximizing utility of consumers in a modern market economy is in fact very similar to the models presented above.

The essence of maximizing total utility is to maximize the utility for every unit of labor input that is needed to produce the goods. In a modern market economy, the labor input becomes the socially necessary labor to produce the goods. As I discussed in the previous chapter, the socially necessary labor to produce the goods is the labor value contained in the final products or services. The key here is to maximize the utility per labor value. To maximize the utility per labor value, the consumer must have complete information about the labor value of a product. This requires the prices of the product to reflect the labor value needed to produce the goods. In short, for each individual to maximize his or her total utility while the society maximizes its total utility, the prices of the goods at the market must reflect the labor value they contain. Only when the prices of goods reflect the necessary labor hours needed to produce the goods can the individual's pursuit of maximization of utility and satisfaction directly result in the maximization of total utility of the economy.

As we discussed above, maximization of a consumer's utility is equivalent to the maximization of utility per labor hour. Now, look at the whole market economy. Imagine the input to a market economy is labor hours, and the output of the market economy is the goods and services that will generate utility. How can we maximize utility? We need to make sure that we maximize output utility relative to each unit of input labor hour. Under this condition, if we increase the input of the system, the output of total utility will increase at the highest efficiency.

THE CASE OF A BRIDGE

For instance, suppose a government decides to build a bridge over a river. There are two ways to build the bridge: one is to use concrete, and the other is to use steel. Assume the bridge has the same utility regardless of which material will be used. The concrete bridge will cost 100,000 labor hours and the steel bridge will cost 50,000 labor hours. To maximize the utility per labor hour, the government chooses to take the steel bridge design, since it only costs half as much as the concrete bridge. Assume U is the total utility for the bridge, then $U/50,000 > U/100,000$ (the numbers are labor hours for each construction method). The utility of the steel bridge per labor hour is twice as high as the utility of the concrete bridge per labor hour. However, when the decision-makers do not have the correct information about how many labor hours will be needed to build the bridge, the decision could be reversed. Say, if the concrete bridge appears to cost 40,000 labor hours, when the actual social cost is 100,000, the government may choose to build a concrete bridge, which will have lower utility per labor value than the steel bridge. Imagine for a given period of time, an economy has only 100,000 labor hours as input; with the correct decision discussed above, two bridges can be built. With the wrong decision, only one bridge can be built. Therefore, when consumers and decision makers do not have correct information about

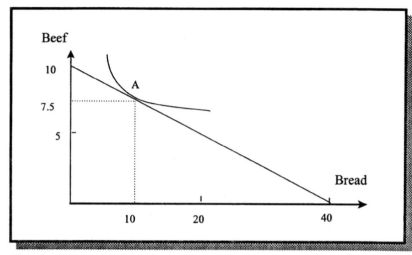

Figure 2.10   Utility Maximization for Alex

the labor value of products and services, wrong decisions can be made, and the maximization of utility becomes impossible. For this reason, it is very important for the price of merchandise to reflect the labor value.

ALEX AND BASIL TWO PERSON MODEL

In the following, I will present a two-persons utility model. This is to illustrate that the maximization of the utility of individuals depends on whether or not the price system can correctly reflect the labor value embedded in the goods or services.

Suppose we have two persons: Alex and Basil. They form an economy. They produce two goods: beef and bread. They have each worked 40 hours. Assume $1 is equivalent to one labor hour. Thus, each of them has made $40 for the given time. We are to maximize their utility. Suppose a loaf of bread takes 1 hour to make; one kilogram of beef takes 4 hour to make.

First we assume the prices of the goods reflect the value of the goods. That is, the price of the bread is $1 per loaf, and the price per kilogram of beef is $4.

Figure 2.10 is the utility curve and purchasing possibility curve for Alex. If Alex chooses to use all his money on beef, he will be able to

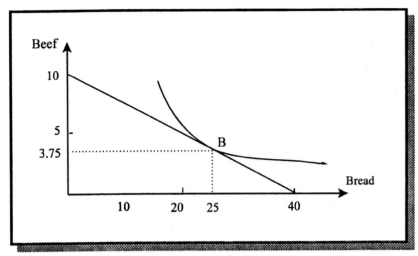

Figure 2.11   Utility Maximization for Basil

purchase $40/$4 = 10 kilograms of beef. If he chooses to use all his money for bread, he will be able to purchase $40/$1=40 loaves of bread. These two points determine the purchasing possibility curve. His indifference curve and his purchasing possibility curve determine the maximum utility point A. At the maximum utility point, he consumes 7.5 kilograms of beef and 10 loaves of bread.

Figure 2.11 is the utility curve and purchasing possibility curve for Basil. If Basil chooses to use all his money on beef, he will be able to purchase $40/$4 = 10 kilograms of beef. If he chooses to use all his money for bread, he will be able to purchase $40/$1=40 loaves of bread. These two points determine the purchasing possibility curve. His indifference curve and his purchasing possibility curve determine the maximum utility point B. At the maximum utility point, he consumes 3.75 kilograms of beef and 25 loaves of bread.

Next, we will show what occurs if the price of the good does not reflect the value of the good. In other words, the price of the bread is not $1 per loaf, and the price per kilogram of beef is not $4. To find out what is going to happen to the total utility for each person, let's study two cases. In the first case, the price of bread increases, while the price of beef decreases. In the second case, both prices decrease. After this analysis, one can easily see that the utility level will be reduced if prices do not reflect the value of the commodities.

FIRST CASE

In the first case, we assume the price of a loaf of bread is $2; and the price of beef is $3 for a kilogram. The change in the price will change the purchasing possibility curve. As a result, it reduces the maximum utility that can be achieved.

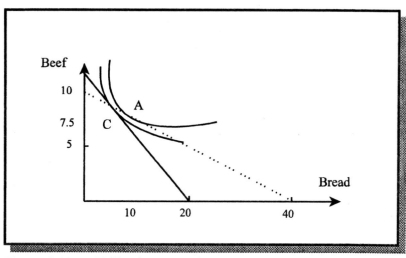

Figure 2.12   Utility for Alex with Incorrect Price

Figure 2.12 is the utility curve and purchasing possibility curve for Alex. If Alex chooses to use all his money on beef, he will be able to purchase $40/3 = 13.3 kilograms of beef. If he chooses to use all his money for bread, he will be able to purchase $40/2=20 loaves of bread. These two points determine the purchasing possibility curve. His indifference curve and his purchasing possibility curve determine the maximum utility point C. At the maximum utility point, he consumes 7 kilograms of beef and 9.5 loaves of bread. This utility level is lower than in the previous case where the prices correctly reflected the value of the goods.

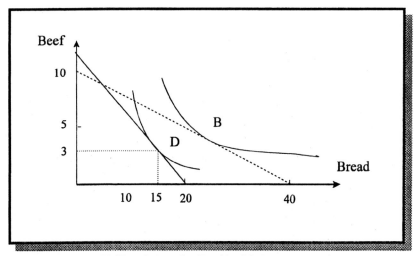

Figure 2.13   Utility Curve for Basil with Incorrect Price

Figure 2.13 is the utility curve and purchasing possibility curve for Basil. If Basil chooses to use all his money on beef, he will be able to purchase $40/3 = 13.3 kilograms of beef. If he were to use all his money for bread, he would be able to purchase $40/2=20 loaves of bread. These two points determine the purchasing possibility curve. His indifference curves and his purchasing possibility curve determines the maximum utility point D. At the maximum utility point, he consumes 3 kilograms of beef and 15.5 loaves of bread. The utility is lower than in the previous case where the prices correctly reflected the value of the goods.

Thus, if the price does not correctly reflect the value of the goods, the total utility level will be reduced for both consumers.

SECOND CASE

In the second case, the prices of both goods decrease. Suppose the price of beef is reduced to $3 per kilogram and the price of bread is reduced to $0.9 per loaf. At these price levels, a new purchasing possibility curve is produced.

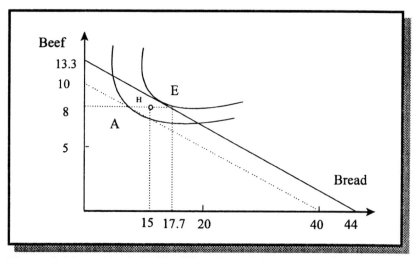

Figure 2.14   Alex's Utility When Both Prices Are Reduced

Figure 2.14 is the utility curve and purchasing possibility curve for Alex. If Alex were to use all his money on beef, he would be able to purchase $40/3 = 13.3 kilograms of beef. If he were to use all his money for bread, he would be able to purchase $40/0.9=44.4 loaves of bread. These two points determine the purchasing possibility curve. His indifference curves and his purchasing possibility curve determine the maximum utility point E. At the maximum utility point, he consumes 8 kilograms of beef and 17.7 [(40 - (3 × 8))/0.9 = 17.7] loaves of bread. The utility level appears higher than in the previous case where prices correctly reflected the value of the goods.

Figure 2.15 is the utility curve and purchasing possibility curve for Basil. If Basil were to use all his money on beef, he would be able to purchase $40/3 = 13.3 kilograms of beef. If he were to use all his money for bread, he would be able to purchase $40/0.9=44.4 loaves of bread. These two points determine the purchasing possibility curve. His indifference curves and his purchasing possibility curve determine the maximum utility point F. At the maximum utility point, he consumes 29 loaves of bread and 4.6 kilograms of beef [(40 - (0.9 × 29))/3 = 4.6].

The utility appears to be higher than in the previous case where the prices correctly reflected the value of the goods.

When the prices of goods correctly reflect the value of the goods, the purchasing possibility curve coincides with the production possibility curve. Therefore, any utility points beyond the purchasing possibility curve (defined with the correct price which reflects the value of the good) are also beyond the production possibility curve. Therefore, those utility points at the right side of the purchasing possibility curve (dotted line production possibility curve in Figure 2.14 and Figure 2.15) defined by the correct price level, which reflect the value of the goods, are not reachable.

In this case, the total bread that Alex and Basil will consume is 17.7 + 29 = 46.7 loaves. The total beef that Alex and Basil will consume is 8 + 4.6 = 12.6 kilograms. However, each loaf of bread takes 1 labor hour to make. Therefore, it takes 46.7 hours to make their bread. It takes 4 hours of labor to produce each kilogram of beef; therefore, 4 × 12.6 = 50.4 labor hours. So, the total labor hours needed to produce

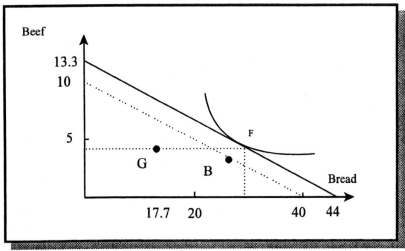

Figure 2.15   Basil's Utility When Both Prices Are Reduced

the goods at the current level of consumption is 50.4 + 46.7 = 97.1 labor hours. We know from the beginning of this analysis, Alex and Basil each put in 40 labor hours. Therefore, it is impossible for them to produce the necessary 97.1 worth of labor hours of goods.

Now, suppose Alex and Basil know the supply of goods may be limited, so they both went out to purchase the beef. Alex purchased 8 kilograms to maximize his utility and Basil went out and purchased 4.6 kilograms of beef. This used up products that are worth 50.4 labor hours. Since 80 hours labor is the total input, the remaining labor hours are 80 - 50.4 = 29.6 labor hours. This suggests there will be only 29.6 loaves of bread available, while the demand is for 46.7 loaves of bread. Suppose each person gets half of what is available (29.6 loaves), about 15 loaves per person. In this case, Alex obtains the higher utility level (Figure 2.14, point H), while Basil's utility level suffers (Figure 15, point G). This situation is very much like that of the old Soviet Union, when people had money to buy beef and bread, but there were not enough goods to supply the demand. In such cases, consumers turn to non-monetary methods to obtain goods. Generally speaking, the utility cannot be maximized. Since we cannot say Alex's gain is more than Basil's loss, the result is somewhat uncertain. However, we know this is not an equilibrium point, since there is money left and no goods are available. This is not a desirable situation for any society. However, if we suppose Alex gets 9.6 loaves of bread and Basil obtains 20 loaves of bread, we will find both parties are worse off than the situation in which the price can correctly reflect the value of the goods. Points A and B in Figures 2.14 and 2.15 are the old utility maximization points in Figures 2.10 and 2.11.

We can conclude that when both prices are lower than the correct price levels that reflect the value of goods, one of the following will happen: both parties are worse off, or one party is much worse off and the other party obtains a higher utility level. In this case, the economy cannot achieve equilibrium. The consumer has money, but there are no goods in the market for them to purchase. None of these situations (where price does not correctly reflect the value of goods) are desirable.

Although, I will not illustrate here, it is easy to imagine what will happen if the prices of both goods are higher than what is correct for them to reflect the price of the goods. The purchasing possibility curve will shift to the left, which reduces the quantity of goods that can be purchased by each consumer. This will certainly reduce the utility level the consumer can achieve.

CONCLUSION OF TWO GOODS AND TWO PERSON MODEL

Thus, if the price does not correctly reflect the value of the goods, the total utility level will be reduced. The above example uses a two persons, two-goods model, but the principle can be generalized into an n goods and m person model, where n and m are any integers larger than 2.

THE AGGREGATE MODEL

Another way to illustrate the basic concept that it is necessary to have the prices of goods reflect the value of the goods is to study the aggregate utility curve with an aggregate purchasing possibility curve. An aggregate utility indifference curve is similar to the utility indifference curve used in our previous models that present a utility indifference curve for an individual consumer. The aggregate utility indifference curve presents the utility indifference curve for society as a whole. Similarly, the aggregate purchasing possibility curve defines the maximum purchasing possibility for the society as a whole.

Suppose we have an economy in which there are billions of consumers and consumption units; this can be a business or a branch of a government. For a two-goods world, there is an aggregate utility indifference curve. Suppose the two goods are chicken and rice. For a given time period, the economy has a total input of 1 billion socially necessary labor hours. Assume one socially necessary labor hour is equivalent to $10. The total output of the economy will be equivalent to $10 billion. Suppose it takes 0.4 labor hour to produce 1 kilogram of chicken, and it takes 0.1 labor hour to produce 1 kilogram of rice. Thus, the correct prices that reflect the value of the goods are $4 per kilogram of chicken ($10 × 0.4 = $4), $1 per kilogram of rice ($10 × 0.1 = $1). Since $10 is equivalent to one socially necessary labor hour, one billion socially necessary labor hours will be equivalent to $10 billion. That is to say, the total compensation for the labor for this given period is $10 billion. If the total $10 billion is spent on chicken, how much can consumers purchase? $10 billion/ $4 = 2.5 billion kilograms of chicken. If the total $10 billion is to be spent on rice, the following amount of rice will be purchased: $10 billion/$1 = 10 billions kilograms. These two numbers determine the purchasing possibility curve intersection point on the horizontal axis and the vertical axis. (Figure 2.16) An aggregate utility indifference curve meets the purchasing possibility curve at point K. Point K is the maximum utility point the society can achieve.

There are three aggregate utility indifference curves in Figure

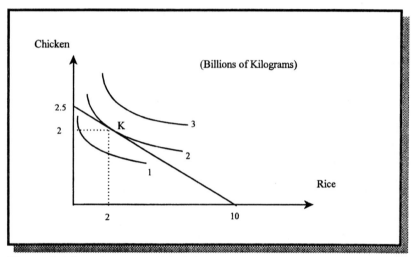

Figure 2.16   Aggregate Model

2.16. They are marked as 1, 2, and 3. Curve 3 has the highest utility level. The indifference curve 1 has the lowest utility curve. The highest utility level this society can achieve with the given purchasing possibility curve is the second aggregate utility indifference curve. Suppose point K corresponds to 2 billion kilograms of chicken. The corresponding point on the horizontal axis is ($10 billion - $4 × 2 billion)/$1 = 2 billion kilograms of rice.

What I will show is if the prices of goods do not correctly reflect the value of the goods, the aggregate utility level will decrease. As a result the society as a whole will enjoy lower utility. That translates to a loss of happiness, of pleasure, and of satisfaction for consumers.

When price does not correctly reflect the value of the goods, the price of the rice is not $1 per kilogram, and the price per kilogram of chicken is not $4 per kilogram. Let's study three cases. In the first case, the price of rice increases, while the price of chicken decreases. In the second case, the price of rice decreases, and the price of chicken increases. In the third case, both prices decrease. After this analysis, readers can easily see that the utility level will be reduced if both prices increase relative to the correct price level.

In the first case, we assume, the price of rice increases to $2 from $1, and the price of chicken decreases to $3 per kilogram from $4. The change of the price will change the purchasing possibility curve. This reduces the maximum utility that can be achieved.

Figure 2.17 is the aggregate utility indifference curve and aggregate purchasing possibility curve for the society. If the society were to use all its money on chicken, it would be able to purchase $10

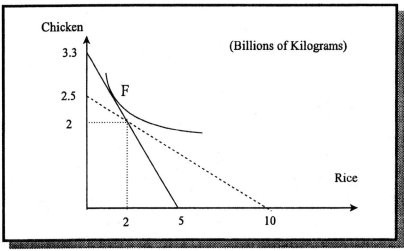

Figure 2.17   Rice Price Up and Chicken Price Down

billion/$3 = 3.33 billion kilograms of chicken. If it were to use all its money for rice, it would be able to purchase $10 billion/$2 = 5 billion kilograms of rice. These two points determine the aggregate purchasing possibility curve (solid line). The aggregate indifference curves and the purchasing possibility curve determine the maximum utility point F. The utility level is higher than in the previous case where the price correctly reflected the value of the goods. However, point F is at the right side of the purchasing possibility curve that is generated when the prices of goods correctly reflect the value of goods. Such a kind of purchasing possibility curve coincides with the production possibility curve. Therefore, any points at the right side of the curve are not reachable at current input and productivity level.

In the second case, the price of rice decreases, and the price of chicken increases.

Figure 2.18 is the utility indifference curve and purchasing

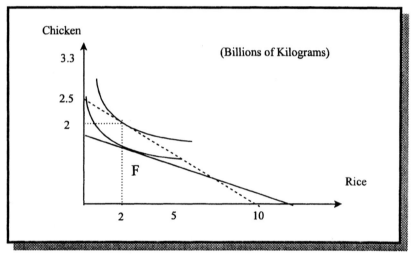

Figure 2.18   Rice Price Down and Chicken Price Up

possibility curve for the society when the price of rice decreases, and the price of chicken increases. Suppose the price of rice decreases to $0.8 per kilogram and the price of chicken increases to $6 per kilogram. If the society were to use all its money on chicken, it would be able to purchase $10 billion/$6 = 1.67 billion kilograms of chicken. If it were to use all its money for rice, it would be able to purchase $10 billion/$0.8 = 12.5 billion kilograms of rice. These two points determine the purchasing possibility curve (solid line in Figure 2.18) under the new distorted pricing system. The aggregate indifference curves and the aggregate purchasing possibility curve determine the maximum utility point F. This maximum utility point F is lower than the maximum utility point obtained when the prices correctly reflect the value of the goods.

Thus, if the price does not correctly reflect the value of the goods, the total utility level will be reduced or the utility point becomes unreachable.

In the third case, the prices of both goods decrease. Suppose the price of chicken is reduced to $3 per kilogram from $4, and the price of rice is reduced to $0.9 per kilogram of rice from $1. At these price levels, a new purchasing possibility curve is produced.

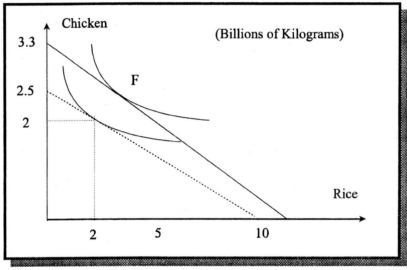

Figure 2.19   Both Rice and Chicken Price Down

Figure 2.19 shows the aggregate utility indifference curve and the aggregate purchasing possibility curve for the economy. If the society were to use all its money on chicken, the society would be able to purchase $10 billion/$3 = 3.3 billion kilograms of chicken. If the society were to use all its money for rice, it would be able to purchase $10 billion/$0.9 = 11.1 billion kilograms of rice. These two numbers determine the aggregate purchasing possibility curve (solid line in Figure 2.19). The aggregate utility indifference curves and the aggregate purchasing possibility curve determine the maximum utility point F. The maximum utility point F is at the right side of the original purchasing possibility curve that is generated when the prices of goods correctly reflect the value of the goods. When the prices of goods correctly reflect the value of the goods, the purchasing possibility curve coincides with the production possibility curve. Therefore, any utility points beyond the purchasing possibility curve defined with the correct price, which reflect the value of the goods, are also beyond the production possibility curve. Therefore, those utility points at the right side of the purchasing possibility curve defined by the correct price level are not reachable.

CONCLUSION OF AGGREGATE MODEL

In summary, the price of goods in a market economy must reflect the true labor value. This is necessary so that when distributed decision makers maximize their own utility or self interest, they can at the same time unintentionally maximize the efficiency of the whole market economy. By improving the utility per social labor hour, the individual decision-makers in an economy will find the least social economic cost to satisfy their needs and wants.

EQUAL EXCHANGE AS THE CONDITION FOR MAXIMUM EFFICIENCY

Two important characteristics of a modern market economy are division of labor and specialization. A product is often made by combining input from many businesses. Consider today's personal computer, for example; the case may be made by company A, the power supply made by company B, the system board made by company C, the hard drive made by company D, the CD ROM drive made by company E, the monitor made by company F, the keyboard made by company G, and the speaker and microphone made by company H. These are some of the physical components that end up in the final product: a computer. On the other side, there are many components used in the processes of development, manufacture, marketing, and sale of the product, which are not visible in the final product, such as technology, management skill, human labor, and capital. Furthermore, in any of the individual computer components listed above, we will find the same pattern repeated in the manufacturing of the keyboard, or speaker, or other components. Each component is composite of many subcomponents made by different manufacturers. This process can go on and on.

Suppose we have a product that is composed of 10 components, and each subcomponent also is composed of 10 subcomponents. So this product will involve 100 subcomponents or companies. Suppose each subcomponent also needs 10 subcomponents, thus the product will actually need 1000 subcomponents or elements to produce. This means there are 1000 contracts or transactions in obtaining the sub-subcomponents. Assume these are all manufactured by different companies.

The task is to have the price of the final product reflect the true labor value. The only way the price of the final product will reflect the labor value is when all the transactions that happen while obtaining the components or inputs necessary to produce the goods are conducted with equal exchange of value. Equal exchange of value means the buyer purchases the goods at the price of the labor value. The transaction is conducted at price levels that reflect the labor value contained in the product or service. Many intermediate products used by industry are also used by consumers, such as personal computers, TVs, VCRs, pens, papers, and furniture, etc. To make sure prices of these products reflect the labor value, it is necessary to hold the principle of equal exchange of value.

Furthermore, these companies are usually not in the same country nor are they on the same continent. Often some of the companies may be in the U.S., while others are in Japan or China. We will later devote special attention to international trade related issues. For now, we assume the division of labor happens only within one economy. In most case, one economy refers to an economy of one country.

Equal exchange of value is the condition necessary to ensure that the final products for consumers meet the requirement for economic efficiency when maximizing the consumer utility. The equal exchange of value is necessary because only under this condition can we expect the final products for consumers or industrial use will carry the correct prices that reflect the socially necessary labor hours that are needed to produce the goods.

MAXIMIZE EFFICIENCY OF PRODUCTION AND OPTIMAL INTEREST RATE

In the subsequent discussion on optimal parameters of the market economy, I will assume there is no taxation or foreign trade of any kind. I will devote special sections to such topics in a later volume of this book.

INTEREST AND INTEREST RATE

Suppose Mr. Williams lent Mr. Lee $100 on the first day of 1990. Mr. Lee agreed to pay back the loan on the first day of the year 1991. How much should Mr. Lee pay back to Mr. Williams? Is it $100?

As we saw earlier, the efficiency of the market requires the equal exchange of value. So if one socially necessary labor hour is equivalent to $10 in 1990 (socially necessary labor hour is also called labor value hours, average labor hour, labor hour or labor hour value), the loan amount of $100 will be equivalent to 10 average labor hours. Suppose on the first day of the year 1991, an average labor hour is equivalent to $11. How much money does Mr. Lee need to repay the loan? According to the equal exchange of value, Mr. Lee has borrowed money that is equivalent to 10 labor value hours; therefore, he should return the same amount of labor value at the end of the year when he repays his loan of $100. Since one average socially necessary labor hour is equivalent to $11 by the first day of 1991, 10 labor value hours would be equivalent to $110. The difference between $110 in return and $100 of initial loan amount is the interest. The interest rate is the amount of interest divided by the initial loan amount. When calculating interest rate, one year of time is often used. The result is often called annual interest rate. According to the above theory, to reach the maximum efficiency an economy must allow interest. The interest must be in an amount that is determined by the rule of the equal exchange of value.

You should note the relationship between labor value in terms of hours and labor value in terms of currency, which is defined in the above discussion.

To put this into a mathematical equation, we have:

$$R = (V(1) - V(0)) /V(0) = V(1)/V(0) - 1 \qquad (2.1)$$

Where:

R: the interest rate

V(0):   one labor hour value in equivalent currency at the beginning of the year

V(1):   one labor hour value in equivalent currency at the end of the year

Putting the above example into this equation, we have

$V(0) = \$10$
$V(1) = \$11$
$R = V(1)/V(0) - 1 = 11/10 - 1 = 10\%$

The interest rate is 10%.

What causes the interest? Where does the interest come from? What determines the amount of interest? There are two major causes that produce interest. One is inflation, and the other is the rate of social productivity improvement. Social productivity refers to the productivity of the whole economy.

Suppose there is no productivity improvement in an economy. Holding other things unchanged, inflation is the sole source of interest. Since the social productivity is unchanged, and assuming there is no change in the distribution of wealth, the average socially necessary labor hour will still buy the same amount of goods at the end of the inflation period as at the beginning of the period. When there is inflation, the general price level rises; so does the monetary equivalent of one labor hour. This is necessary so that the average labor hour has the same purchasing power at the beginning of the inflation period as it has at the end of inflation periods. This requires that the monetary equivalent of the average socially necessary labor hour, in terms of currency, increases at the same speed as the inflation. Suppose the average labor hour in the economy is equivalent to $10 per hour on the first day of a year; exactly one year later, it is equivalent to $12 for the average labor hour. The difference between the $12 and $10 per hour average labor is the interest. The interest rate is (12-10)/10=20%. This is also the inflation rate. Therefore, in this case the interest rate is equal to the inflation rate.

The following illustrates why the inflation rate will be equal to the interest rate. As there is no productivity improvement over the year in the economy, at the end of the year the output per labor hour will remain the same as it was in the beginning of the year. Say five goods will be produced by the average labor hour. Suppose the average price of the goods is $10 each at the start of the year. Exactly one year later the average price becomes $11. This is a 10% inflation. Therefore, the total worth of goods produced by the average labor hour at the start of the year is $10 × 5 = $50. In other words, the one average labor hour is equivalent to $50. At the end of year, the total worth of goods produced by the average labor hour is $11 × 5 = $55. That is to say, the one labor hour at the end of the year is equivalent to $55. What if a bank lends $50 to XYZ corporation at the beginning of the year? How much should XYZ corporation repay to the bank at the end of year? If we apply the equal exchange of value rule to our case, we can easily conclude that XYZ corporation should repay an amount of $55.00. The reason is that the $55 at the end of the year and the $50 at the beginning of the year are equivalent to the same amount of labor value.

Note the difference in the following two sentences. (1) The average labor hour cost $50. (2) The average labor hour is equivalent to $50. The difference arises because sometimes in an economy, the equilibrium of exchange does not rest on equal exchange of value. As the salmon model in Chapter One illustrates, only under perfect market conditions (a competitive market with full employment), can labor get paid according to its value. For a market economy without full employment, laborers are usually underpaid relative to the labor value they produce. Therefore, it is preferred to use the phrase "the average labor hour is equivalent to $50." This is a more precise expression.

Similarly, social productivity improvement also induces interest. Suppose there is no inflation, and total labor hour input to an economy stays the same. When there is no inflation, the inflation rate equals zero. As the social productivity improves, more goods and services will be produced with the same amount of labor hour input. Assuming the distribution of wealth does not change, then the average purchasing power of the average labor value hour will enjoy a purchasing power increase at the same rate as the social productivity increase rate. When the inflation rate is zero, the income measured in currency per labor value hour will increase at the same speed as the social productivity growth rate. Suppose one labor value hour is $100 on the first day of the year; exactly one year later, one labor value hour becomes $106, while the inflation rate equals zero. This increase represents the social productivity improvement. Applying the equal exchange of value to this case, if Mr. Smith borrows $100 at the beginning of the year and return the loan exactly one year afterwards, Mr. Smith should return not only $100 but also an additional $6 extra to make the exchange an equal exchange of value. In this case the social productivity growth rate equals 6%. In conclusion, the social productivity growth rate equals the interest rate if we hold equal exchange of value when there is no inflation.

When the inflation rate is zero, why should the productivity growth rate of the economy be equal to the interest rate? The output per labor hour will increase as the productivity increases. Say 5 typical goods will be produced by the average labor hour at the beginning of the year and by the end of the year, the average labor hour produces 7 goods. Since there is no inflation, the price of typical goods does not change. Say the price is $10 throughout the year. The 5 goods produced by an average labor hour at the beginning of the year are worth $10 × 5 = $50. The 7 goods produced at the end of the year will be worth $10 × 7 = $70. That is to say, at the beginning of the year, one labor hour is equivalent to $50, while at the end of the year, one labor hour is equivalent to $70. The productivity growth rate and interest rate can be calculated as:

Productivity growth rate = 7/5 - 1 = 40%
Interest rate = 70/50 - 1 = 40%

This process shows that the productivity growth rate is equal to the interest rate when the inflation rate is zero.

To combine the effect of both inflation and the productivity growth rate, consider the following model which puts these two factors into one equation.

Suppose we study a one-year period of time. There is a 10% inflation during this one year period. We further suppose there is a 15% productivity improvement made in the economy during this one-year period. To reflect the 15% of productivity improvement in the economy, we suppose one labor hour produces 100 typical products at the beginning of the year, and produces 115 typical products at the end of the year. To take 10% inflation into consideration, we assume the price of the typical goods at the beginning of the year is $1 each, while at the end of the year it becomes $1.10 each. In monetary terms, how much is one labor hour worth at the start of the year? And how much is it worth at the end of the year? At the start of the year, it is $1 × 100 = $100. At the end of the year, it is $1.1 × 115 = $126.50.

From this we know that at the start of the year one labor hour is equivalent to $100, while at the end of the year, one labor hour is equivalent to $126.50. In other words, if Mr. Johnson borrows $100 at the beginning of the year, he should repay $126.50 at the end of the year. In this case, the interest rate is $126.50/100 - 1 = 26.5%. To convert this calculation into a formula, we can use variables instead of numbers, as in the following paragraph.

To reflect the "S" of productivity improvement in the economy, we suppose one labor hour produces "Q" typical products at the beginning of the year, and produces "Q(1 + S)" typical products at the end of the year. To take "I" inflation into consideration, we assume the price of the typical goods at the beginning of the year is "$D" each, while at the end the year it becomes "$D × (1 + I)" each. In monetary terms, how much is one labor hour worth at the start of the year? And how much is it worth at the end of the year? At the start of the year, it is $D × Q. At the end of the year, it is calculated by multiplying price by the number of goods produced by one labor hour:

$$\$D \times (1 + I) \times Q(1 + S)$$

Applying Equation 2.1, we have the following:

$$\text{Interest rate} = [\$D \times (1 + I) \times Q(1 + S)]/[\$D \times Q] - 1$$
$$= (1 + I)(1 + S) - 1$$

$$R = (1 + S)(1 + I) - 1 \qquad (2.2)$$

where:

> R: interest rate
> S: social productivity growth rate
> I: inflation rate of the economy

In the above equation, R is the optimal interest rate. The reason I call it the optimal interest rate is because the relationship described in the equation presents the optimal condition. Only when an economy operates with such a relationship among interest rate, social productivity growth rate, and inflation rate, can the equal exchange of value happen in that economy. As we discussed above, only when the equal exchange of value happens, can the average price of goods reflect the value of the goods, which is a condition for utility maximization for both consumers and business-users of products.

What exactly is "I" in the above equation? Consider an economy as a black box. We put in labor hours and the black box produces goods and services consumers need and want. In this context, the inflation rate "I" in the above equation refers to the change in price of those goods and services that are bought or used by consumers. The inflation rate should not include price changes of machinery used in the manufacturing process, since machinery are not directly used by consumers to satisfy their needs and wants. Everything that is directly used by consumers to satisfy their needs and wants should be included in the calculation of the inflation rate "I". This should include goods directly purchased by consumers, such as, a private aircraft, house, boat, automobile, a toll road, food, or entertainment. The consumer price index is the actual economic data that best fits this definition.

What exactly is "S" in the above equation? In the same context as discussed above, the productivity change rate refers to the productivity of an economy in terms of producing consumer goods and services relative to the input, which is the socially necessary labor hours used in producing those goods and services. GDP (Gross Domestic Product) is the economic indicator closest to the "S" in the above equation for an economy that does not have productivity growth rate statistics.

If a government wants to improve the efficiency of its economy, the government should adopt an economic policy that will change the interest rate of the economy to be equal to the optimal interest rate discussed above. As one of the many conditions for maximum economic efficiency, the interest rate should be made equal to the optimal interest rate.

EFFICIENCY MAXIMIZATION AND OPTIMAL PROFIT

Investors want more profit out of the business in which they invest. The stock price will go up if the company makes an unexpectedly larger profit. From the investors' point of view, the larger the profit the better. So how can there be an optimal profit? Usually a higher than average profit is the result of excellent management, marketing, technical advance, and innovation. The pursuit of profit is one of the major motivations in a market economy. The analysis below does not suggest a limit should be put on how much profit can be made, it is to find a relationship between profit and other economic parameters, such as interest rate, social productivity growth rate, and inflation rate when economic efficiency is maximized. When the profit rate has a certain relationship with some other economic parameters, the whole economy will operate at the highest efficiency.

As we consider this topic, please bear in mind that all the major deductions are based on the conclusions established at the beginning of this chapter. Equal exchange of value is a necessary condition for the maximum efficiency of a market economy. I will also assume that supply equals demand in this market economy. In other words, we will be studying the equilibrium point of the market. The optimal parameters of the economy refer to the equilibrium point of the market.

Typically, there are millions and millions of businesses in an economy. Let's pick one which represents the average business in an economy. By studying an average business, I will try to expose the relationship between the maximization of efficiency of a market economy and the requirement for such efficiency maximization on the behavior of the profit.

It is commonly observed that business has two kinds of inputs: one is labor, and the other is capital. Material is a form of capital input for the purpose of this discussion. The output is whatever services or products the business produces, such as food service, iron, or steel.

When there is no inflation, the productivity growth rate of the economy is equal to the rate of increase in monetary terms per equivalent socially average labor hour (Equation 2.2). Suppose there is a 15% productivity improvement in the economy during the period. If $10 is equivalent to one socially average labor hour at the start of a period, then at the end of the period $11.50 will be equivalent to one socially average labor hour ($10 × (1 +15%) = 11.5). This is to be explained below.

To illustrate, let's suppose the economy uses 1 million labor hours to produce 1 million goods per day at the beginning of a year; because there is a 15% productivity improvement, at the end of the year the same million labor hours will be able to produce 15% more goods. This is a total of 1.15 million goods. Further, suppose at the beginning of the year $10 is equivalent to one socially average labor hour. Because there is no inflation, the general price level does not change; thus we have:

$10 × 1 million labor hour /1 million goods = V(1) × 1 million labor hour/1.15 million goods

The left side is the general price level at the beginning of the year. The right side of the equation is the general price level at the end of the year. They are equal since we know the inflation rate is zero. At the end of the year $V(1) is equivalent to one socially necessary average labor hour.

$$10 × 1.15 = V(1)$$
$$V(1) = \$11.50$$

To put this into a formula:

$$V(1) = V(0)(1 + S) \tag{2.3}$$

Where:

V(0):   monetary equivalent to one labor hour at the beginning of the period

V(1):   monetary equivalent to one labor hour at the end of the period

S: percentage of productivity improvement in the economy over the period

What will be the average profit rate (equilibrium profit rate) if the economy is operating at the ideal peak economic efficiency? As I discussed above, if the economy is to operate at peak economic efficiency, goods must be changed with equal value at equilibrium.

EXAMINE AN AVERAGE BUSINESS (REFRIGERATOR MODEL)

Suppose we examine an average business in an economy for a one-year period. At the start of the year, one labor hour is equivalent to $10. There is no inflation. That is, the inflation rate is zero. We further suppose there is a 15% productivity improvement in the economy over this one-year period of time. Since we are examining an average business, this business also enjoys an average productivity improvement of 15% over the year.

Suppose at the start of the year $5000 capital and $500 of labor can produce 100 refrigerators. The $5000 capital here only refers to the value of the capital that transfers to the final products. (For example, if a machine of $1000 can produce 1000 refrigerators in its useful time, it will transfer $1 to each new refrigerator manufactured. For 100 refrigerators, we would say $100 of capital has been used, not the $1000 of capital.) How much are the 100 refrigerators produced at the start of the year in terms of labor value? As we assumed at the beginning of this analysis, one labor hour is equivalent to $10. Based on this, $5000 capital will be equivalent to 500 labor hours, and $500 of labor is equivalent to 50 labor hours. Thus, 550 labor hours are used in producing the 100 refrigerators. As the productivity improves 15% over the one year period, by the end of the year the same 550 labor hours will be able to produce 115 refrigerators ($100 \times (1 + 15\%)$). The price of the refrigerators at the beginning of the year is ($5000 + $500)/100 =$55. The total revenue at the end of the year is $55 \times 115 = $6325.

Profit is made during the process of reaching equilibrium (Chapter 1). The surplus value is a transitory phenomenon and is generated by productivity improvement. In a perfect competitive market with full employment, the surplus value will become zero at equilibrium.

As there is no inflation, at the end of the year the price of the refrigerators does not change. It will be still at $55.00. In the above discussion (Equation 2.3), we conclude that the monetary equivalent to one socially necessary labor hour increases at a rate equal to the average social productivity growth rate of the economy. That is to say, if $10 is equivalent to one labor hour at the start of the year, after a 15% productivity improvement at the end of the year, $10 \times (1 + 15\%) = $11.50 is equivalent to one labor hour (Equation 2.3). Based on this, we can apply the equal exchange of value to the capital. That is to say, if the capitalist invested 500 labor hours at the start of the year, he should be able to get 500 labor hours at the end of the year, assuming the operation only lasted one year. Therefore, at the end of the year, the investors should get $11.5 × 500 = $5750. The difference between the $5000 invested at the start of the year and this amount is the profit. The profit is $5750 - $5000 = $750. The profit rate is $750/$5000 = 15%. It is the same as the average productivity growth rate of the economy. Similarly, we apply the equal exchange of value to the labor. If 50 labor hours are used at the end of year in producing 100 refrigerators, the 50 labor hours should get compensated at $11.50 × 50 = $575. Comparing this with the $500.00 compensation laborer should get at the beginning of the year for the same amount of labor input, we find it increases by $75. When consider the sum of what the investor should get and what the laborer should get, we have $5750 + $575 = $6325. This is the same number as the total revenue at the end of the year we calculated above.

To put the conclusion from the above analysis into a formula, we have:

P = S
P: average profit rate
S: socially average productivity growth rate

Table 2. 3

	Beginning T1	End of period T2
Capital used (in labor hours)	K	K
Labor used (in labor hours)	Lb	Lb
Currency equivalent of one labor hour	V(0)	(1 + S)V(0)

This above relationship can also be obtained by the following analysis which uses variables (Table 2.3) instead of numbers.

The profit rate and wage change rate can be calculated as:

Profit rate
= Capital (\$) at T2/Capital (\$) at T1 - 1

$$\frac{(S + 1)V(0)K}{V(0)K} - 1 = (S + 1) -1 = S$$

This equation shows that the profit rate equals the social productivity growth rate. We can also calculate the wage increase rate by using the variables in the table.

Wage increase rate = Labor (\$) T2/labor (\$) at T1 - 1

$$\frac{V(0)(S + 1)Lb}{V(0)Lb} - 1 = (S + 1) -1 = S$$

Wage increase rate = S

This equation shows that the wage increase rate equals the social productivity growth rate, when the inflation rate is zero and the economy is operating at ideal conditions. In other words, the rate of increase in monetary compensation to average labor hour is equal to the socially average productivity growth rate when inflation is zero.

Bear in mind that we are studying the equilibrium point of exchange. The equation presents the equilibrium points of two parameters; one is the profit rate, and the other is the socially average productivity growth rate. Only when the equilibrium points of the two parameters are equal can the economy operate at its peak efficiency.

The socially average productivity improvement is the same as the average productivity growth rate of the economy. It is just stated in different words.

Monetary compensation for the labor hour should increase at the same rate as the socially average productivity growth rate. This is necessary so that equal exchange of value can happen. Only when the rate of increase in monetary compensation for the average labor hour equals the socially average productivity growth rate can the economic system operate at its peak efficiency.

In the above, we studied a model with an average business that enjoys the same productivity improvement as that of the economy in the same period of time. What happens to the business that has less or more productivity improvement than the productivity growth rate of the economy?

EXAMINE A BUSINESS THAT DOES NOT MAKE ANY PRODUCTIVITY IMPROVEMENT (STUDENT CHAIR)

Assumptions: The business is a typical business in its line of product. In other words, what this business experiences is what the average business experiences in this industry or its line of product.

Inflation rate = 0

Time = One year period

Productivity growth rate of the economy = 15%

One socially necessary labor hour is equivalent to $10 at the beginning of the year.

In the previous discussion, we know $V(1) = V(0)(1 + S)$. Based on this equation, we know one socially necessary labor hour is equivalent to $11.5 at the end of the year.

$$V(0) (1 + S) = 10 \times (1 + 15\%) = 11.50$$

Suppose at the start of the year $5000 capital and $500 labor can produce 100 student chairs. The $5000 capital here only refers to the value of the capital that transfers to the final products. (For example, if a machine of $1000 can produce 1000 student chairs in its useful time, it will transfer $1 to each new student chair manufactured. For 100 student chairs, we would say $100 of capital has been used, not the $1000 of capital.) How much did the 100 student chairs produced at the start of the year cost in terms of labor value? As we assumed at the beginning of this analysis, one labor hour is equivalent to $10. Based on this, $5000 capital will be equivalent to 500 labor hours, and $500 of labor is equivalent to 50 labor hours. Thus, $(500 + 50) = 550$ labor hours are used in producing the 100 student chairs.

The price of the student chairs at the beginning of the year is ($5000 + $500)/100 = $55. Remember, at equilibrium the surplus value is zero. (Refer to Chapter 1 for a detailed discussion). The total revenue at the start of the year is $55 × 100 = $5,500. As there is no inflation, at the end of the year, the general price level of the economy does not change. However, some prices may go up and others go down. Since this is not the average business, the price of its output may not stay the same.

If $10 is equivalent to one labor hour at the start of the year, after a 15% productivity improvement at the end of the year:

$$\$10 \times (1 + 15\%) = \$11.50$$

is equivalent to one labor hour. Based on this, we can apply the equal exchange of value to the capital. That is to say, if the capitalist invested 500 labor hours at the start of the year, the total return including the investment amount should be 500 labor hours at the end of the year as we assume the operation only lasted one year. Therefore, at the end of the year, the investors should get $11.5 × 500 = $5750. The difference, between the $5000 invested at the start of the year and this amount, is the profit. The profit is $5750 - $5000 = $750. The profit rate is $750/$5000 = 15%. It is the same as the average productivity growth rate of the economy. Similarly, we can apply the equal exchange of value to the labor. If the 50 labor hours are used at the end of year in producing 100 student chairs, the 50 labor hours should get compensated at $11.50 × 50 = $575. This represents an increase of $75 when comparing this with the $500.00 compensation laborer should get at the beginning of the year for the same amount of labor input. If we take a sum of what the investor should get with what the laborer should get, we have $5750 + $575 = $6325. This should be the total revenue for the 100 student chairs produced at the end of the year. From this information, we can calculate the price of the student chairs. It is $6325 /100 = $63.25. This is a 15% increase, since $55 × (1 + 15%) = $63.25. From this we see that if the business does not make any productivity improvement, the price of its product should increase at the same rate as the productivity growth rate of the economy.

CONCLUSION FOR BUSINESS WITHOUT PRODUCTIVITY IMPROVEMENT

Condition: In an ideal economy, with zero inflation, a business makes no productivity improvement over the concerned period.

$$P = S$$
$$C = S$$

Where:

P: the profit rate of the business

S: productivity growth rate of the economy

C: price level change rate for the product in an industry or business that does not make any productivity improvement

The price of the products of this business should increase at the same rate as the rate of productivity improvement of the economy. Only then will the economy operate at its peak efficiency.

A BUSINESS WITH TWICE THE AVERAGE PRODUCTIVITY GROWTH RATE

Examine a business that makes productivity improvement twice as fast as the whole economy. In the above, we have studied an average business, a business which makes no productivity improvement. In the following we will examine a business that makes twice the rate of productivity improvement as that of the economy.

Assumptions:

The business is a typical business in its line of product. In other words, what this business experiences is what the average business experiences in this industry or line of product.

Inflation rate = 0

Time = One year period

Productivity growth rate of the economy = 15%

Productivity growth rate of the business = 30%

One socially necessary labor hour is equivalent to $10 at the beginning of the year.

In the previous discussion, we know $V(1) = V(0)(1 + S)$. Based on this equation, we know one socially necessary labor hour is equivalent to $11.50 at the end of the year.

Suppose at the start of the year $5000 of capital and $500 of labor can produce 100 CPUs. (CPU standards for Central Processing Unit, a computer chip.) The $5000 capital here only refers to the value of the capital that transfers to the final products. (For example, if a machine of $1000 can produce 1000 CPUs in its useful time, it will transfer $1 to each new CPU manufactured. For 100 CPUs, we would say $100 of capital has been used, not the $1000.00 of capital.) How much are the 100 CPUs produced at the start of the year in terms of labor value? As we assumed at the beginning of this analysis, one labor hour is equivalent to $10. Based on this, $5000 capital will be equivalent to 500 labor hours, and $500 of labor is equivalent to 50 labor hours. Thus, 550 labor hours are used in producing the 100 CPUs.

The price of the CPUs at the beginning of the year is ($5000 + $500)/100 = $55. The total revenue at the start of the year is $55 × 100 = $5500. As there is no inflation, at the end of the year, the general price level of the economy does not change. However, some prices may go up and others go down. Since this is not the average business, the price of its output may not stay the same.

If $10 is equivalent to one labor hour at the start of the year, after a 15% productivity improvement of the economy at the end of the year $10 × (1 + 15%) = $11.50 is equivalent to one labor hour. Based on this, we can apply the equal exchange of value to the capital. That is to say if the capitalist invested 500 labor hours at the start of the year, he should be able to get 500 labor hours at the end of the year as we assume the operation only lasted one year. Therefore, at the end of the year, the investors should get $11.50 × 500 = $5750. The difference, between the $5000 invested at the start of the year and this amount, is the profit. The profit is $5750 - $5000 = $750. The profit rate is $750/$5000 = 15% . It is the same as the average productivity growth rate of the economy. Similarly, we can apply the equal exchange of value to the labor. If the 50 labor hours are used at the end of year to produce 100 CPUs, the 50 labor hours should get compensated for at $11.5 × 50 = $575. Compare this with the $500.00 compensation laborer should get at the beginning of the year for the same amount of labor input, we find the compensation increases by $75, a 15% increase.

When we take a sum of what the investor should get and what the laborer should get, we have $5750 + $575 = $6325. This should be the total revenue of the 100 CPUs produced at the end of the year. From this information, we can calculate the price of the CPUs. Note, as the productivity increases 30% at this business, the same amount of labor can now produce 30% more product. The output for the same input increases from 100 to 130 CPUs. The price of the CPUs is $6325/130 = $48.70. This is an 11% decrease in price, since ($55 - $48.70)/$55= 11%.

The reduced price is equal to:

new price

= original price $\times (1+ S)/(1+ B)$

= $55(1+15\%)/(1+30 \%)$

= $48.70

Where:

S: the productivity growth rate of the economy

B: the productivity growth rate of the business, product, or industry

price change rate $= (1 + S)/(1 + B) - 1$

This equation can be obtained by the following analysis (Table 2.4) with variables.

ending price $= V(0)(1 + S)(K + Lb)/[Q(1 + B)]$

beginning price $= V(0)(K + Lb)/Q$

price change rate = ending price/beginning price - 1

$= (1 + S)/(1 + B) - 1$

Table 2. 4

Period	Beginning	Ending
Output quantity	Q	$Q(1 + S)$
Capital used (labor hours)	K	K
Monetary amount (per labor hour)	V(0)	$V(0) (1 + S)$
Labor used (labor hours)	Lb	Lb

CONCLUSION FOR A BUSINESS WITH TWICE THE AVERAGE PRODUCTIVITY GROWTH RATE (CPU MODEL)

Condition: In an ideal economy, with zero inflation, a business makes more productivity improvement than the rate of productivity improvement of the economy over the concerned period.

P = S

C = (1 + S)/(1 + B) - 1   (2.4)

where:

P: average profit rate

S: socially average productivity growth rate.

C: price level change rate

Then, the price of the products of this business should change at the rate as C in Equation 2.4. Only then will the economy operate at its peak efficiency.

APPLICATION EXAMPLE

This is an interesting formula, but does it work for price increases? Here I put the student chair model into the formula.

C = (1 + S)/(1 + B) - 1
  = (1 + 15%)/(1 + 0%) - 1
  = 1.15% - 1 = 15%

The result is great. The 15% means a 15% increase. It is the same result we get in the previous model. This means we have just found a general formula for price change.

Putting this into general terms, we have the three equations below:

B = (1 + S)/(1+ C) -1
C = (1 + S)/(1 + B) -1
P = (1+ C)(1+ B) - 1

Where:

C: price change rate for a product

S: the productivity growth rate of the economy

B: the productivity growth rate of the business, or product
          or, industry

EXAMPLE 2.1

The price change rate equation is a very useful equation. This
example illustrates how it can be used to estimate the productivity
growth rate of an industry?

For a given period of time, the price of computer memory chips
falls 40% in the U.S., while the U.S. economy is moving at a 2%
productivity growth rate for the same period of time (all data is
hypothetical). The inflation rate is zero. We can plug the data into the
above equation. This gives us an estimate of the productivity growth
rate of the memory chip industry. Plugging in the data:

$$C = (1 + S)/(1 + B) - 1$$
$$-40\% = (1 + 2\%)/(1 + B) - 1$$
$$60\% = (1 + 2\%)/(1 + B)$$
$$60\% (1 + B) = 1.02$$
$$1 + B = 1.02 / 0.6$$
$$B = 1.02/0.6 - 1 = 70\%$$

Thus, we know the memory chip industry is enjoying a 70%
productivity improvement over the concerned period. The reason we can
use this formula to estimate the productivity improvement is that the
real world economy is very close to the ideal economy. It is certain that
there will be errors, since the real world economy is not ideal.

Similarly, if we know the productivity change of an industry
and its price change, we can estimate the productivity change rate of the
economy.

EXAMPLE 2.2

Assume the inflation rate is zero. If the price of house is
declining 5% for a period of time, while the productivity of the housing
industry has increased 8%, what is the estimated productivity growth
rate of the economy?

Transform equation (2.4) to: $S = (1 + C)(1 + B) - 1$
$$S = (1 - 5\%)(1 + 8\%) - 1 = 2.6\%$$
Answer: the productivity of the economy has improved 2.6%.

THE INTRODUCTION OF INFLATION INTO THE EQUATION

First we need to discuss what happens to the monetary terms equivalent of the socially necessary labor hour with the introduction of inflation.

Suppose there is 12% inflation, and 15% productivity improvement in the economy during the period. If $10 is equivalent to one socially necessary labor hour at the start of a period, then at the end of the period, how much will the equivalent of one socially necessary labor hour be?

To illustrate, let's suppose the economy uses 1 million labor hours to produce 1 million goods per day at the beginning of a year. Because there is a 15% productivity improvement, at the end of the year the same one million labor hour will be able to produce 15% more goods. That is 1.15 million goods. Further, suppose at the beginning of the year $10 is equivalent to one socially average labor hour. Because there is 12% inflation, the general price level will rise by 12%, thus we have:

($10 × 1 million labor hour/1 million goods)(1 + 12%) = V(1) × 1 million labor hour/1.15 million goods

The left side is the general price level at the beginning of the year times the inflation factor. The right side of the equation is the general price level at the end of the year. They are equal since the left side is the price level at the beginning of the year times the inflation factor, and the left side will have the same price as the end of the year. At the end of the year V(1) is equivalent to one socially necessary average labor hour. Let Q be the total quantity produced at the beginning of the period, we turn the above equation into:

$$V(0)(1 + I)/Q = V(1)/[Q(1 + S)]$$
$$V(1) = V(0)(1 + S)(1 + I) \qquad (2.5)$$

Where:

V(0):   monetary equivalent to one labor hour at the beginning of the period

V(1):   monetary equivalent to one labor hour at the end of the period

S: percentage of productivity improvement in the economy over the period

I: inflation rate of the economy

$$V(1) = 10 \times (1 + 15\%)(1 + 12\%) = 10 \times 1.288 = \$12.88$$

Answer: at the end of the period, $12.88 is equivalent to one labor hour.

HEATER MODEL

First, let's examine an average business that has the same productivity growth rate as the economy.

Assumptions:

Inflation rate = 12%

Time = One year period

Productivity growth rate of the economy = 15%

One socially necessary labor hour is equivalent to $10 at the beginning of the year.

In the previous discussion, we know:

$$V(1) = 10 \times (1 + 15\%)(1 + 12\%) = 10 \times 1.288 = \$12.88$$

Based on this equation, we know one socially necessary labor hour is equivalent to $12.88 at the end of the year.

Suppose at the start of the year $5000 of capital and $500 of labor can produce 100 heaters. The $5000 capital here only refers to the value of the capital that transfers to the final products. (For example, if a machine of $1000 can produce 1000 heaters in its useful time, it will transfer $1 to each new heater manufactured. For 100 heaters, we would say $100 of capital has been used, not the $1000 of capital.) How much are the 100 heaters produced at the start of the year in terms of labor value? As we assumed at the beginning of this analysis, one labor hour is equivalent to $10. Based on this, $5000 of capital will be equivalent to 500 labor hours, and $500 of labor is equivalent to 50 labor hours. Thus, 550 labor hours are used in producing the 100 heaters.

The price of the heaters at the beginning of the year is ($5000 + $500)/100 = $55. The total revenue at the start of the year is $55 × 100

= \$5500. As there is 12% inflation, at the end of the year the general price level of the economy does increase 12%, and so does the price of heaters of this business.

If \$10 is equivalent to one labor hour at the start of the year, after a 15% productivity improvement and 12% inflation, at the end of the year \$12.88 is equivalent to one labor hour. Based on this, we can apply the equal exchange of value to the capital. That is to say, if the capitalist invested 500 labor hours at the start of the year, he should be able to get 500 labor hours equivalent monetary compensation at the end of the year as we assume the operation only lasted one year. Therefore, at the end of the year, the investors should get \$12.88 × 500 = \$6440. The difference, between the \$5000 invested at the start of the year and this amount, is the profit. The profit is \$6440 - \$5000 = \$1440. The profit rate is \$1440/\$5000 = 28.8%. Putting this into our equation format:

> The profit rate
> = (1 + 15%)(1 + 12%) - 1
> = 1.288 - 1 = 28.5%

> Profit rate
> = [V(1) - V(0)]/V(0)
> = (1 + S)(1+ I) - 1

Similarly, we apply the equal exchange of value to the labor. If 50 labor hours are used at the end of year in producing 115 heaters, the 50 labor hours should get compensated at \$12.88 × 50 = \$644. Compare this with the \$500.00 compensation laborer should get at the beginning of the year for the same amount of labor input. The compensation increase rate should be:

($644 - $500)/$500 = 28.8%

To present this in a general equation:

> Labor compensation increase rate
> = [V(1) - V(0)]/V(0)
> = (1 + S)(1+ I) - 1

If we take a sum of what the investor should get and what the laborer should get, we have $6440 + $644 = $7084. This should be the total revenue of the 115 heaters produced at the end of the year. From this information, we can calculate the price of the heaters. It is $7084/115 = $61.60. This is a 12% increase, since $55 × (1 + 12%) = $61.60.

From this we see that if a business makes the same productivity improvement, the price of its product will increase at the same rate as the inflation rate of the economy.

Table 2. 5

Period	Start	End
Capital (labor hours)	K	K
Labor (labor hours)	Lb	Lb
Monetary equivalent per labor hour	V(0)	V(0)(1 + S)(1 + I)

Using variables, we have the following analysis (Table 2.5):

profit rate = [V(0)(1 + S)(1 + I)K]/[V(0)K] - 1
profit rate = P = (1 + S)(1 + I) - 1

wage change rate = [V(0)(1 + S)(1 + I)Lb]/[V(0)Lb] - 1
wage change rate = L = (1 + S)(1 + I) - 1

price change rate = ending price/starting price - 1

Because:
starting price = V(0)(K + Lb)/Q
ending Price = [V(0)(1 + S)(1 + I)(K + Lb)]/[Q(1 + S)]

Thus:
price change rate = C = (1 + I) - 1 = I

CONCLUSION OF HEATER MODEL

Condition: In an ideal economy, a business makes the same productivity improvement as the economy over the concerned period.

P = (1 + S)(1 + I) - 1
L = (1 + S)(1 + I) - 1
C = I

Where:

P: profit rate
L: wage change rate
C: price change rate

The economic parameter should have the above relations, only then will the economy operate at its peak efficiency.

CAR SEAT MODEL

Let's examine a business that has made no productivity improvement, while the economy is enjoying a 15% productivity improvement. Assumptions:

The business is a typical business in its line of product. In other words, what this business experiences is what the average business experiences in this industry or its line of product.

Inflation rate = 12%

Time = One year period

Productivity growth rate of the economy = 15%

One socially necessary labor hour is equivalent to $10 at the beginning of the year.

In the previous discussion, we know:

V(1) = 10 × (1 + 15%)(1 + 12%) = 10 × 1.288 = $12.88

Based on this equation, we know one socially necessary labor hour is equivalent to $12.88 at the end of the year.

Suppose at the start of the year $5000 of capital and $500 of labor can produce 100 car seats. The $5000 capital here only refers to the value of the capital that transfers to the final products. (For example, if a machine of $1000 can produce 1000 car seats in its useful time, it will transfer $1 to each new car seat manufactured. For 100 car seats, we would say $100 of capital has been used, not the $1000 of capital.) How much are the 100 car seats produced at the start of the year in terms of labor value? As we assumed at the beginning of this analysis, one labor hour is equivalent to $10. Based on this, $5000 capital will be equivalent to 500 labor hours, and $500 of labor is equivalent to 50 labor hours. Thus, 550 labor hours are used in producing the 100 car seats.

The price of the car seats at the beginning of the year is ($5000 + $500)/100 = $55. The total revenue at the start of the year is $55 × 100 = $5500. As there is 12% inflation, at the end of the year, the general price level of the economy increases 12%. Since the car seat maker has not made productivity improvement, it is most likely that its product will have a price increase than the inflation rate of the economy

If $10 is equivalent to one labor hour at the start of the year, after 15% of productivity improvement and 12% inflation, at the end of the year $12.88 is equivalent to one labor hour. Based on this, we can apply the equal exchange of value to the capital. That is to say, if the capitalist invested 500 labor hours at the start of the year, he should be able to get 500 labor hours at the end of the year, as we assume the operation only lasts one year. Therefore, at the end of the year, the investors should get $12.88 × 500 = $6440. The difference between the $5000 invested at the start of the year and this amount is the profit. The profit is $6440 - $5000 = $1440. The profit rate is $1440/$5000 = 28.8%.

Put this into equation format:

The profit rate = (1 + 15%)(1 + 12%) - 1 = 1.288 - 1 = 28.5%

Profit rate = [V(1) - V(0)]/V(0) = (1 + S)(1 + I) - 1

Similarly, we apply the equal exchange of value to the labor. If 50 labor hours are used at the end of year in producing 100 car seats, the 50 labor hours should get paid for $12.88 × 50 = $644. Compare this with the $500.00 compensation laborer should get at the beginning of the year for the same amount of labor input, and we have the compensation increase rate:

($644 - $500)/$500 = 28.8%

Present this in a general equation:

labor compensation increase rate
= [V(1) - V(0)]/V(0)
= (1 + S)(1 + I) - 1

We take a sum of what the investor should get and what the laborer should get, we have $6440 + $644 = $7084. This should be the total revenue of the 100 car seats produced at the end of the year. From this information, we can calculate the price of the car seats. It is $7084 /100 = $70.84. This is 28.8% increase, since $55 × (1 + 12%)(1 + 15%) = $70.84

Table 2. 6

Period	Start	End
Quantity of the product	Q	Q
Labor (labor hour)	Lb	Lb
Monetary Equivalent per labor hour	V(0)	V(0)(1 + S)(1 + I)
Capital (labor hour)	K	K

Put this into a more general term equation:

price increase rate of this product
= C
= (1 + S)(1 + I) - 1

From this we see that if the business make no productivity improvement, the price of its product will increase at the above rate.
    The following explains how the equations above are obtained.

profit rate = [V(0)(1 + S)(1 + I)K]/[V(0)K] - 1
profit rate = P = (1 + S)(1 + I) - 1

wage change rate = [V(0)(1 + S)(1 + I)Lb]/[V(0)Lb] - 1
wage change rate = L = (1 + S)(1 + I) - 1
price change rate = ending price/starting price - 1

Because:

starting price = V(0)(K + Lb)/Q
ending Price = [V(0)(1 + S)(1 + I)(K + Lb)]/Q

Thus:

price change rate =
$$C = (1 + S)(1 + I) - 1$$

CONCLUSION OF CAR SEAT MODEL

Condition: In an ideal economy, a business makes no productivity improvement, while the economy has made productivity improvement over the concerned period.

$$L = P = C = (1 + S)(1 + I) - 1$$

Where:

L: labor Wage change rate
P: profit rate
C: price change rate for a product
S: percentage productivity improvement in the economy over the period
I: inflation rate of the economy

CELLULAR PHONE MODEL

Third we examine a business that has made 25% productivity improvement, while the economy is enjoying 15% productivity improvement. Assumptions:

The business is a typical business in its line of product. In other words, what this business experiences is what the average business experiences in this industry or its line of product.

Inflation rate = 12%

Time =One year period

Productivity growth rate of the economy = 15%

One socially necessary labor hour is equivalent to $10 at the beginning of the year.

In the previous discussion, we know
$$V(1) = 10 \times (1 + 15\%)(1 + 12\%) = 10 \times 1.288 = \$12.88$$
Based on this equation, we know one socially necessary labor hour is equivalent to $12.88 at the end of the year.

Suppose at the start of the year $5000 capital and $500 of labor can produce 100 cellular phones. The $5000 capital here only refers to the value of the capital that transfers to the final products. (For example, if a machine of $1000 can produce 1000 cellular phones in its useful time, it will transfer $1 to each new cellular phone manufactured. For 100 cellular phones, we would say $100 of capital has been used, not the $1000 of capital.)

How much is the 100 cellular phones produced at the start of the year in terms of labor value? As we assumed at the beginning of this analysis, one labor hour is equivalent to $10. Based on this, $5000 capital will be equivalent to 500 labor hours, and $500 of labor is equivalent to 50 labor hours. Thus, 550 labor hours are used in producing the 100 cellular phones.

The price of the cellular phones at the beginning of the year is ($5000 + $500)/100 = $55. The total revenue at the start of the year is $55 × 100 = $5500. As there is 12% inflation, at the end of the year, the general price level of the economy increases 12%. Since the cellular phone maker has made 25% productivity improvement, it is most likely that its product will have a price increase rate lower than the inflation rate of the economy.

If $10 is equivalent to one labor hour at the start of the year, after 15% of productivity improvement and 12% inflation, at the end of the year $12.88 is equivalent to one labor hour. Based on this, we can apply the equal exchange of value to the capital. That is to say, if the capitalist invested 500 labor hours at the start of the year, he should be able to get 500 labor hours at the end of the year as we assume the operation only lasts one year. Therefore, at the end of the year, the investors should get $12.88 × 500 = $6440. The difference between the $5000 invested at the start of the year and this amount is the profit. The profit is $6440 - $5000 = $1440. The profit rate is $1440/$5000 = 28.8%. Put this into equation format:

profit rate
$$= (1 + 15\%)(1 + 12\%) - 1$$

= 1.288 - 1 = 28.5%

profit rate = $(1 + S)(1 + I) - 1$

Similarly, we apply the equal exchange of value to the labor. If 50 labor hours are used at the end of year in producing 100 cellular phones, the 50 labor hours should get paid for $12.88 × 50 = $644. Compare this with the $500.00 compensation laborer should get at the beginning of the year for the same amount of labor input, we have the compensation increase rate as:

($644 - $500)/$500 = 28.8%

Present this in a general equation:

Table 2. 7

Period	Start	End
Quantity of the product	Q	Q(1 + B)
Labor (labor hour)	Lb	Lb
Monetary Equivalent per labor hour	V(0)	V(0)(1 + S)(1 + I)
Capital (labor hour)	K	K

labor compensation increase rate
= $(1 + S)(1 + I) - 1$

We take a sum of what the investor should get and what the laborer should get, we have $6440 + $644 = $7084. This should be the total revenue of the 125 cellular phones produced at the end of the year. (100 × (1 + 25%) = 125) Remember there is 25% productivity improvement on cellular phone production. From this information, we can calculate the price of the cellular phones. It is $7084/125= $56.672.

This is 3% increase in price, since

$55 × (1 + 12%)(1 + 15%)/(1 + 25%) = $55 × 1.0304 = $56.672.

Put this into a more general term equation

price increase rate of this product
= C
= (1 + S)(1 + I) /(1 + B) - 1
(1 + C)(1 + B) = (1 + S)(1 + I)

From this we see that if the business makes some productivity improvement, the price of its product will increase or decrease at the above rate.

The above equations can also be obtained by the following analysis (Table 2.7).

profit rate = [V(0)(1 + S)(1 + I)K]/[V(0)K] - 1
profit rate = P = (1 + S)(1 + I) - 1

wage change rate = [V(0)(1 + S)(1 + I)Lb]/[V(0)Lb] - 1
wage change rate = L = (1 + S)(1 + I) - 1

price change rate = ending price/starting price - 1

Because:

starting price = V(0)(K + Lb)/Q
ending Price = [V(0)(1 + S)(1 + I)(K + Lb)]/[Q(1 + B)]

Thus:

price change rate =
C = (1 + S)(1 + I)/(1 + B) - 1
(1 + C)(1 + B) = (1 + S)(1 + I)

CONCLUSION OF CELLULAR PHONE MODEL

Condition: In an ideal economy, a business makes productivity improvement, while the economy also makes productivity improvement over the concerned period.

$$L = P = (1 + S)(1 + I) - 1$$

or

$$1 + L = 1 + P = (1 + C)(1 + B) = (1 + S)(1 + I)$$

Where:

C: price change rate for the product
S: the productivity growth rate of the economy
B: the productivity growth rate of the business, or product or industry
I: inflation rate of the economy
L: wage change rate
P: profit rate of the business in concern

In conclusion, in an ideal economy, only when the economic parameters have the above relations, can the economy operate at peak economic efficiency.

MODELS, CONDITIONS, AND FINDINGS

Table 2.8 shows the featuring conditions and major findings for each model we discussed above. The last major finding is the general case, which makes the other models a special case. By setting the conditions of the last major finding equation, we can obtain all the other equations from refrigerator model to car seat model.

Table 2. 8

Model	Featuring Conditions	Major Findings
Refrigerator	$I = 0, B = S$	$P = S, L = S$
Student Chair	$I = 0, B = 0$	$P = S, C = S, L = S$
CPU	$I = 0, B > S$	$P = S, L = S$ $C = (1 + S)/(1 + B) - 1$
Heater	$I > 0, S > 0, B = S$	$P = L = (1 + S)(1 + I) - 1$ $C = I$
Car Seat	$I > 0, S > 0, B = 0$	$P = L = C = (1 + S)(1 + I) - 1$
CELLULAR PHONE	$I > 0, S > 0, B > 0$	$1 + L = 1 + P = (1 + C)(1 + B)$ $= (1 + S)(1 + I)$

APPLICATION EXAMPLES

Let's see how we can use the above equations. The limitations of these equations are that the model deals with a closed and ideal economy. It does not take international trade into consideration. It deals with parameters at their equilibrium point in an ideal economy. We can use the equations from the above analysis to the real world economy, because the real world market economy is very close to the ideal economy.

EXAMPLE 2.3

Suppose in 1998, China's economy has experienced 7% of productivity improvement, 1.5% deflation. The price of steel has fallen 5% (All data here are hypothetical). We want to know the productivity growth rate of the steel industry.

$$B = (1 + S)(1 + I)/(1 + C) - 1$$
$$B = (1 + 7\%)(1 - 1.5\%)/(1 - 5\%) - 1$$
$$= 10.9\%$$

The productivity of the steel industry is 10.9%. This answer will be correct if the major economy parameters also meet the requirement of an ideal economy, such as P = S.

EXAMPLE 2.4

Suppose a business executive Mr. Young wants to estimate the price of a product 5 years down the road. He estimates the economy will make 6% productivity improvement per year. The inflation rate is 1%. The manufacture of this product will experience about 4% productivity per year over the next 5 years.

$$C = (1 + S)(1 + I)/(1 + B) - 1$$

$$S = 1.06 \times 1.06 \times 1.06 \times 1.06 \times 1.06 - 1 = 33.8\%$$
$$I = 1.01 \times 1.01 \times 1.01 \times 1.01 \times 1.01 - 1 = 5.1\%$$
$$B = 1.04 \times 1.04 \times 1.04 \times 1.04 \times 1.04 - 1 = 21.6\%$$

$$C = (1 + 0.338)(1 + 0.051)/(1 + 0.216) - 1$$
$$= 15.6\%$$

The price of the product is expected to increase 15.6% under a perfect competitive market in an ideal economy.

SUMMARIZE THE FINDINGS OF THIS SECTION

The following equations represent the optimal economic parameters and their optimal relations. Only when the economic parameters of an economy have the following relations, can the economy operate at its peak economic efficiency. When an economy operates at peak economic efficiency, its economic parameters must have the following relations:

$$[V(1) - V(0)]/V(0) + 1$$
$$= R + 1$$
$$= L + 1$$
$$= P + 1$$
$$= (C + 1)(1 + B)$$
$$= (1 + S)(1 + I)$$

Where:

C: price change rate for the product

S: the productivity growth rate of the economy

B: the productivity growth rate of the business, or a product or an industry

I: inflation rate of the economy (consumer goods and services)

L: labor monetary compensation increase rate

R: interest rate

I: inflation rate of the economy

P: profit rate of a business or industry

V(1):   monetary equivalent of one labor hour at the end of period

V(0):   monetary equivalent of one labor hour at the beginning of the period

SUMMARY OF CONCLUSIONS

1. Marginal utility of the last unit of goods diminishes as more quantity of goods is consumed. Given utility curve characterized as diminishing marginal utility; the increase in total utility will at the same time decrease the marginal utility. While a decrease in the marginal utility suggests increase in quantity consumed, therefore it will increase the total utility, as long as the marginal utility is not negative.

2. For a given budget constraint (purchasing possibility curve), the total utility will be maximized when the marginal utility per cost is equalized.

3. The theory of exchange value in mainstream economics believes marginal utility determines the price. This is incorrect.

4. The total utility of consumers can be maximized, only if the prices of commodities correctly reflect the value of the goods, which is the socially necessary labor hours needed to reproduce the goods.

5. An economy can operate at its peak economic efficiency only if goods are exchanged by the rule of equal exchange of value. The word "goods" refers to things involved with exchange, such as capital, labor, money, and services.

6. Profit and interest are necessary so that equal exchange of value can be upheld. They are necessary so that the economy can operate at maximum efficiency.

7. When an economy is operating at its peak economic efficiency, the economic parameters will have the following relations.

$$V(1) = V(0)(1 + S)(1 + I)$$

$$[V(1) - V(0)]/V(0) + 1$$
$$= R + 1$$
$$= L + 1$$
$$= P + 1$$
$$= (C + 1)(1 + B)$$
$$= (1 + S)(1 + I)$$

Where:

C: price change rate for the product

S: the productivity growth rate of the economy

B: the productivity growth rate of the business, or a product or an industry

I: inflation rate of the economy (consumer goods and services)

L: labor monetary compensation increase rate

R: interest rate

P: profit rate of a business or industry

$V(1)$:   monetary equivalent of one labor hour at the end of period

$V(0)$:   monetary equivalent of one labor hour at the beginning of the period

CHAPTER 3

OPTIMAL PARAMETERS FOR REAL ECONOMY

In Chapter Two, we discussed the optimal economic parameters for an ideal economy. Although the real world economy is very close to the ideal economy, the optimal economic relationship presented in an ideal economy may not hold true for the real world economy. The real world economy is an imperfect world. It is an imperfect world, because: (1) the real world has unemployment; (2) labor compensation increase rate is lower than the ideal labor compensation increase rate (Chapter Two); and (3) some markets are not perfect competitive markets. There are dysfunctional markets (Chapters One and Four) in the real world economy.

The objective of this chapter is to find the optimal economic parameters and optimal economic relationship in the imperfect world by introducing a wage compensator. Because the real world actual labor compensation increase rate is less than the optimal labor compensation increase rate for the ideal economy, the optimal economic relationship established in Chapter Two based on an ideal economy must be modified so that equal exchange of value still holds true in the imperfect economic world. Without this modification, the optimal economic relationship for the ideal economy does not present the optimal economic relationship for the real world economy.

WAGE RATE

The nominal profit growth rate is usually higher than the average labor hour compensation growth rate in the real world economy. Unemployment reduces the hourly labor compensation growth rate so that it is less than what it would be in an ideal economy. There are some major factors that determine the amount of compensation for the laborer.

1.   Collective bargaining is often practiced by trade or labor unions. Usually, blue-collar workers organize to demand better pay, thus pushing up wages. However, businesses are not likely to give in since they can hire cheaper labor from the labor market.

2.   A limited supply of skilled workers can push up their own salary level. This is why CEOs, top scientists, and top engineers are well paid. From 1995 to 1997, there was a very high demand for computer-related technical professionals in the U.S. The compensation for this group of people grew at a rate higher than that of inflation and productivity combined. As technology and specialization develop, the level of the division of labor also increases. This creates a demand for professional

people in special skilled markets. An increase in division of labor puts pressure on businesses to increase pay for specially skilled workers due to the limited supply of these workers.

3.   Compensation is rigid. If there is a 5% inflation, workers will expect their compensation to increase by at least 5% so that their standard of living does not decrease. It is difficult for labor compensation to go down, but easy for it to go up. If a company cuts compensation, it will usually experience decreased morale and an increased employee turnover rate.

In the early years of an industrial revolution, workers are needed mostly for their muscles. As division of labor increases, a higher and higher percentage of workers are needed not for their muscles, but for their brains and knowledge. In the early years of an industrial revolution, workers do not have much power to ask for a wage increase, since unskilled labor is usually oversupplied. The division of labor and the demand for professional knowledge and skill have given labor more and more power in bargaining for higher wages. From this, we can conclude:

(A)   In the early years of an industrial revolution, workers have no power to demand compensation; therefore, the capitalists set wages at levels they want. It is, therefore, most likely that wages increase at a rate much less than the rate of profit.

(B)   As society develops, a skilled labor force will have more bargaining power; therefore, the difference between P (profit rate) and L (the compensation increase rate) will decrease over centuries for skilled and professional laborers.

We can conclude from the above discussion that the following will be the real world reality:

real world $L < (1 + S)(1 + I) - 1$

COMPARING REAL AND IDEAL WAGE RATES

Figure 3.1 illustrates the difference between ideal and real labor compensation increase rates. The horizontal axis represents percentage. When the real labor compensation increase rate is equal to the ideal labor compensation increase rate, the difference between the two is zero. When it is not zero, it suggests that one of these rates be higher than the other. For instance, for the year 1980 a point of -6.3 on the chart in Figure 3.1 suggests the real labor wage (hourly pay) increase rate was 6.3% lower

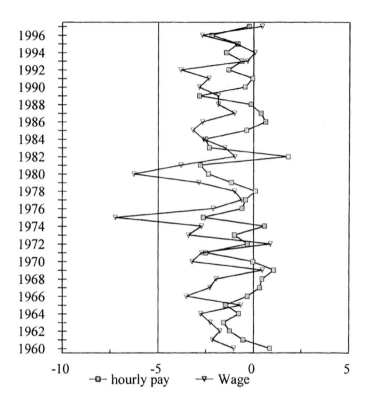

Figure 3.1   The Difference (Y) Between Ideal and Real Labor Compensation Change Rate

Ideal L = (1 + S)(1 + I) - 1

Y = Ideal L - Real L = (1 + S)(1 + I) - 1 - Real L

Each of the two curves illustrates the difference between the change in rate of ideal labor compensation and the real labor compensation.

Source: (U.S.) Economic Report of the President, 1999.

S: Output per hour of all persons in business sector. Table B-50.

I: Annual inflation rate. Changes in consumer price indexes for commodities and services. Table B-64.

L: (1).Hourly pay: Compensation per hour business sector, table B-50.

(2).Wage: Average weekly earnings, total private. Percentage change from year earlier. B-47.

than the ideal labor wage increase rate. There are two curves in the Figure 3.1. One is based on data from compensation per hour, and the other is from average weekly earnings. As discussed above, the real world L is often less than the ideal L (compensation increase rate). The average labor compensation increase rate is about 1 to 2 percent less than the ideal labor compensation increase rate on an average year. Figure 3.1 provides evidence that supports the conclusion that the labor compensation increase rate is less than the ideal labor compensation increase rate discussed in Chapter Two. Only when an economy has full employment can the real labor compensation increase rate be equal to the ideal labor compensation increase rate (Chapter One).

THE OPTIMAL ECONOMIC PARAMETERS

We have discovered optimal economic parameters for the ideal economy, but the real world is not an ideal economy. Therefore, the relations established among optimal parameters in the ideal economy may not be true for the real world economy. The real world economy is an imperfect world. In this section, we will introduce optimal parameters for the imperfect world.

Assume we study a firm for a given period, from T1 to T2 (Table 3.1). The quantity produced in T1 is Q. The quantity produced at T2 is $Q(1 + B)$, where B is the productivity growth rate of the firm. The "input" in terms of labor hours includes capital and labor used in the production process. The monetary equivalent per labor hour is "$V(0)$" at the beginning of the period. From Chapter 2, we know that the monetary equivalent per labor hour at the end of the period is $V(0)(1 + S)(1 + I)$, where "S" is the productivity growth rate of the economy, and "I" is the inflation rate of the economy. However, in the real world, the wage increase rate is lower than the ideal compensation increase rate most of the time. As we discussed in the earlier, when the economy has unemployment, the wage increase rate does not comply with the rule of equal exchange of value. Therefore, we subtract a number, Δ, to arrive at the real world number. Here, Δ is called the wage compensator.

We now apply the law of equal exchange of value in the imperfect world in order to find the optimal relationships among economic parameters. By this law, one labor hour capital invested at T1 should have the same value as the total return of the capital (one labor hour) at T2. When we say the goods should be exchanged according to the equal exchange value at T1 and T2, we imply that at T1 and T2 the economic system is at equilibrium. Only when an economic system is at equilibrium can goods be exchanged according to the equal exchange of value.

Table 3.1

Time	T1	T2
Quantity produced	Q	$Q(1 + B)$
Input (capital and labor) (labor hours)	Input	Input
Monetary equivalent per labor hour	$V(0)$	$V(0)[(1+S)(1+I) - \Delta]$

One labor hour capital at T1 is :
$V(0)$
One labor hour capital at T2 is:
$V(0)[(1 + S)(1 + I) - \Delta]$
Therefore, the profit rate is:
$P = $ (one labor hour capital at T2)/(one labor hour capital at T1) $- 1$
$= (1 + S)(1 + I) - \Delta - 1$
$1 + P = (1 + S)(1 + I) - \Delta$ (3.1)
Since in essence the interest rate R and profit rate P are the same, thus, $R = P$ (Chapter 1 and Chapter 2). Similarly, one labor hour input at T1 should have the same value as one labor hour at T2.

One labor hour labor input at T1 in monetary terms:
$V(0)$
One labor hour labor input at T2 in monetary terms:
$V(0)[(1 + S)(1 + I) - \Delta]$
Therefore, the wage change rate from T1 to T2 is:
$= L$
$=$(One labor hour labor input at T2)/(One labor hour labor input at T1) -1

$= [(1 + S)(1 + I) - \Delta] - 1$

$1 + L = (1 + S)(1 + I) - \Delta$ (3.2)

      The price at T1 and T2 can be calculated as the following:

Price at T1:

      $V(0)$Input$/Q$

Price at T2:

      $V(0)[(1 + S)(1 + I) - \Delta]$ Input$/[Q(1 + B)]$

The price change rate is:

      price change rate

      $= C$

      $=$ (price at T2)/(price at T1) - 1

      $= [(1 + S)(1 + I) - \Delta]/(1 + B) - 1$

Thus,

      $(1 + C)(1 + B) = (1 + S)(1 + I) - \Delta$ (3.3)

SUMMARY OF THE OPTIMAL PARAMETERS FOR THE REAL WORLD ECONOMY

      The following equations illustrate the Law of Optimal Parameters for the Real World Economy – a set of optimal relations in the imperfect world.

      $V(1) = V(0)[(1 + S)(1 + I) - \Delta]$

      $1 + R = (1 + S)(1 + I) - \Delta$

      $1 + P = (1 + S)(1 + I) - \Delta$

      $1 + L = (1 + S)(1 + I) - \Delta$

      $(1 + C)(1 + B) = (1 + S)(1 + I) - \Delta$

                                        (3.4)

Where:

      Δ: wage compensator

      C: price change rate for the product

      S: productivity growth rate of the economy

      B: productivity growth rate of the business, or a product or an industry

      I: inflation rate of the economy (consumer goods and services)

L: labor monetary compensation increase rate
R: nominal interest rate
P: profit rate of a business or industry, or the average profit
          rate of the economy (nominal profit rate)
V(1):   monetary equivalent of one labor hour at the end of the
          period
V(0):   monetary equivalent of one labor hour at the beginning of
          the period

In the imperfect world, the economy will operate at peak economic efficiency if economic parameters have the above relationships. When all the parameters are at optimal value, the following holds true:

$$1 + R = 1 + P = 1 + L$$

This equation illustrates the result of an optimized economy. Before an economy reaches optimal condition, this equation does not hold true. Δ can also be considered a measurement of how close a real world economy is to the ideal economy.

Among the many variables listed above, only one variable can be given or set by an outside force (i.e., a central bank). This variable is the nominal interest rate. It is an exogenous variable. (Figure 3.2) All other variables are determined by the economic system itself. They are called the endogenous variables. Endogenous variables are determined by the market economic system.

The following two equations, which deal with R and P, are obtained by assuming the equal exchange of value at T1 and T2. In other words, the assumption for these equations is that profit rate and interest rate are at equilibrium at T1 and T2.

$$1 + R = (1 + S)(1 + I) - \Delta$$
$$1 + P = (1 + S)(1 + I) - \Delta$$

$$(3.5)$$

The following equation does not rely on the equilibrium assumption; therefore, it is also applicable to nonequilibrium situations.

$$(1 + C)(1 + B) = (1 + S)(1 + I) - \Delta$$

$$(3.6)$$

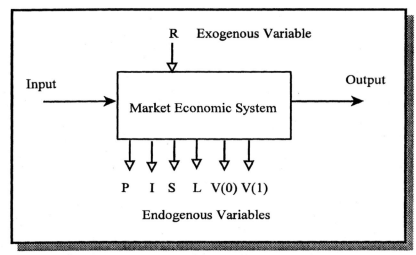

Figure 3.2 Endogenous and Exogenous Variables

Figure 3.2 only illustrates the economic parameters we discussed so far, other economic parameters not shown in Figure 3.2 will be discussed in a later volume.

POLICY IMPLICATIONS

From the above conclusion, we know that when an economy is operating at its peak economic efficiency, it must comply with the Law of Optimal Economic Parameters for the Real World Economy. If an economy has its economic parameters conforming to this Law, it will operate at peak economic efficiency.

From the above optimal economic parameters, we can suggest the following policy recommendations:

1. First, the central bank or government agency should not use the interest rate to control the inflation rate, or to prevent capital from leaving the country. Instead, the government or central bank should set the interest rate to be equal to the optimal interest rate according to the law of optimal parameters for the real world economy.
   Because:

$1 + R = (1 + S)(1 + I) - \Delta$
$1 + L = (1 + S)(1 + I) - \Delta$
Therefore:
$R = L$
The central bank should set the (nominal) interest rate equal to the average labor compensation increase rate.

2.   Economists, governments, or central bank planners should develop new strategies to contain inflation, to stimulate economy, or to prevent capital from leaving the country, so that they do not meddle with the interest rate.

3.   Because the optimal economic parameter is, $L = P = R$, the government should monitor these parameters, and when necessary intervene with economic policy to bring the three parameters as close as possible to this equation.

APPLICATION EXAMPLES

EXAMPLE 3.1

Why is the U.S. economic growth rate higher from 1960 to 1969 than from 1980 to 1989 or from 1990 to 1997? Table 3.2 shows that

Table 3.2

Average Productivity Growth Rate	Percentage
1960-1969	3.19
1970-1979	2.04
1980-1989	1.23
1990-1997	1.01

Source: U.S. Economic Report of the President, February 1999. Table B-50 Output per hour business sector.

during the 60s, the average economic productivity growth rate in the U.S. was 3.19% per year; it was 2.04% in the 70s; 1.23% in the 80s; and

1.01% in the 90s.

Although many factors can contribute to the productivity growth rate, the interest rate plays an important role in determining the efficiency of an economy in the imperfect world. When the nominal interest rate deviates from the optimal interest rate in the imperfect world, the efficiency of the economy is reduced, and the productivity growth rate also decreases (Figure 3.3).

As we examine Figure 3.3, we find that during 1960-1968, the interest rate in the U.S. deviated very little from the optimal interest rate for the real world economy. After 1974, the nominal interest rate consistently deviated from the optimal interest rate by more than 2%. From 1960 to 1970 the U.S. interest rate was within 1% of optimal interest rate according to the Law of Optimal Parameters for the Real World Economy, except for the year 1968. Examine Tables 3.2 and 3.3. The productivity

Table 3.3   Productivity Growth Rate

Year	S	Year	S	Year	S	Year	S
1960	1.7	1970	2	1980	-0.3	1990	0.7
1961	3.5	1971	4.3	1981	1.8	1991	0.6
1962	4.7	1972	3.3	1982	-0.5	1992	3.4
1963	3.9	1973	3.2	1983	3.2	1993	0.1
1964	4.6	1974	-1.7	1984	2.5	1994	0.6
1965	3.5	1975	3.5	1985	1.6	1995	0.3
1966	4	1976	3.4	1986	2.6	1996	2.7
1967	2.2	1977	1.7	1987	-0.1	1997	1.7
1968	3.4	1978	1.1	1988	0.7		
1969	0.4	1979	-0.4	1989	0.8		

Source: U.S. Economic Report of the President, February 1999.

growth rate in the 90s is about 2% lower than it was in the 1960s. This suggests that if the U.S. interest rate had been set to the optimal interest rate according to the Law of Optimal Parameters for the Real World Economy, the U.S. productivity growth rate per year could have been 2% higher. By applying this theory, the U.S. productivity growth rate can improve 216% (3.19%/1.01% -1 = 216%)(Table 3.2). This theory is applicable to any market economy. We can predict that if an economy adopts the Law of Optimal Parameters for the Real World Economy, its average productivity growth rate will be 2% higher, and its economic

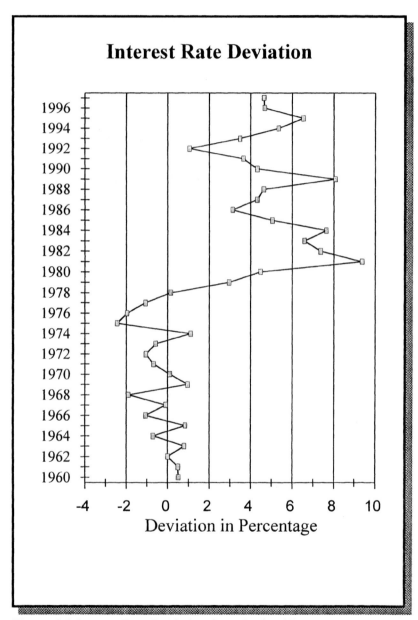

Figure 3.3 Interest Rate Deviation from Optimal Rate
Interest Rate Deviation = Interest Rate - Optimal Interest Rate for the Real
World Economy
Sources: U.S. Economic Report of the President, February 1999.

growth rate can be improved as much as 216%. If all the economies of the world adopt this theory and set interest rates according to the Law of Optimal Parameters for the Real World Economy, the world economic growth rate per year could be 2% higher than it is now, and the world productivity growth rate could be improved as much as 216%.

Table 3.4

Year	Average Deviation
1960 - 1969	0.738
1970 - 1979	1.212
1980 - 1989	6.059
1990 - 1997	4.214

Source: U.S. Economic Report of the President, February 1999.

Table 3.4 represents the average deviation of the interest rate from the optimal interest rate for each decade. The 1980s had the worst average deviation 6.059%. From the year 1990 to 1997, the average deviation was 4.214%. This is the second worst period, however, the productivity growth rate is the lowest of the four periods. The low efficiency of the 1980s may have influenced the 1990s.

EXAMPLE 3.2

If an economy has the following conditions, what is the optimal interest rate? How much is Δ?

Productivity growth rate of the economy $S = 7\%$
Inflation of the economy $I = -0.02\%$
Labor average compensation increase rate $L = 4\%$

Because $R = L$
$R = 4\%$
Because $1 + L = (1 + S)(1 + I) - \Delta$
$\Delta = (1 + S)(1 + I) - L - 1$

$$= 1.07 \times 0.98 - 4\% - 1$$
$$= 0.86\%$$

Answer:

The optimal interest rate is 4%, and $\Delta = 0.86\%$. The central bank or monetary authority should set the interest rate to 4%.

Example 3.3

Let us assume that in 1997 China had the following hypothetical economic data: Employed laborer growth rate was 1.6%. Among the total employed labor force, 80% were farmers. The farmers' income grew at 4.2%, and the non-farmer labor force enjoyed a 6% income growth rate. The inflation rate was -1.2%. GDP growth was 8.5%. What was the optimal interest rate?

Because $R = L$

We need to estimate the average labor income growth rate.

$$L = (4.2\% \times 80\%) + (6\% \times 20\%)/(100\% + 1.6\%)$$
$$= 4.49\%$$

Thus:

$$R = L = 4.49\%$$

Answer: The optimal interest rate is 4.49%. In other words, the central bank should set the interest rate to 4.49%. The cost of capital to business should be 4.49%.

Example 3.4

Suppose an economy has $L = 4.49\%$ in 1997. In a perfect competitive market, if an industry enjoys a 6% productivity growth rate, what will the price change rate be for its product?

Because

$$(1 + C)(1 + B) = (1 + S)(1 + I) - \Delta$$
$$1 + L = (1 + S)(1 + I) - \Delta$$

$(1 + C)(1 + B) = 1 + L$
Thus
$(1 + C)(1 + 6\%) = 1 + 4.49\%$
$1 + C = 0.9857$
$C = -1.424\%$

Answer: The price of the industry will decrease 1.424% over the year.

SUMMARY OF CONCLUSIONS

1.   The real world economy is different from the ideal economy in employment and labor compensation growth rate. Thus, we need to introduce a wage compensator, Δ.

2.   The Law of Optimal Parameters for the Real World economy:

$V(1) = V(0)[(1 + S)(1 + I) - \Delta$

$(1 + C)(1 + B) = (1 + S)(1 + I) - \Delta$

$1 + R = (1 + S)(1 + I) - \Delta$

$1 + P = (1 + S)(1 + I) - \Delta$

$1 + L = (1 + S)(1 + I) - \Delta$

Where:

Δ: wage compensator

C: price change rate for the product

S: the productivity growth rate of the economy

B: the productivity growth rate of the business, or a product or an industry

I: inflation rate of the economy (consumer goods and services)

L: labor monetary compensation increase rate

R: interest rate (nominal interest rate)

P: profit rate of a business or industry, or the average profit rate of the economy (nominal profit rate)

$V(1)$:   monetary equivalent of one labor hour at the end of the period

$V(0)$:   monetary equivalent of one labor hour at the beginning of the period

3.   The monetary authority or central bank should set the interest rate according to the Law of Optimal Parameters for the Real World economy. That is to set the interest rate equal to L.

4. Δ may be used to measure how close an economy is to the ideal economy.

5.   The following equation does not rely on the equilibrium assumption, therefore it is applicable to nonequilibrium situations.

$(1 + C)(1 + B) = (1 + S)(1 + I) - \Delta$

CHAPTER 4

PRICE THEORY AND OPTIMAL PARAMETERS

INTRODUCTION

In the previous chapters, I discussed equal exchange of value, optimal profit rate, optimal labor income growth rate, and how these are related to economic efficiency. It would be really nice if the real world market could automatically achieve the optimal economic parameters without government intervention. This chapter examines how the real world market reality works for and against optimal economic parameters. We will find, in most cases, that the free market system works in terms of moving the economy toward optimal economic efficiency. By discovering the defects of the market system, we can develop a more accountable economic policy for government economic intervention. With the correct understanding of the operations of the market economic system, we will be able to develop proper economic policy. We can significantly improve the efficiency of an economy with proper economic policy. When an economy is operating at its peak economic efficiency, we can expect a higher economic growth rate than we can of an economy in a less efficient state.

The free market economic system is an economic system without government intervention. The pure free market economic system no longer exists in the world since the American government's intervention in the Great Depression of the 1930s. Today, almost every country and regional government is engaged in some kind of economic manipulation, and most governments are trying to run their economy to some degree in an attempt to avoid economic disasters such as a major financial crisis or a depression. The U.S. economic system is not a pure free market economic system. The pure free market economic system is undesirable.

Today, most economists will agree that the managed market economy is the best route to economic growth, stability, efficiency and prosperity. The managed market economy is a reality today, and it is the future. One of the aims of economic theory is to provide guidance to economic policymakers on how to successfully manage a market economy.

HOW DO CONSUMERS MAXIMIZE UTILITY IN THE REAL WORLD?

To parallel with the thought path of Chapter Two, we start with consumer utility maximization. Economists have created many mathematical models to describe and simulate how consumers behave in an economy. The term used to describe consumers' satisfaction and pleasure is *utility*. In economic models, a consumer is assumed to have perfect rationality in making a decision about how, when, what, and where to consume or purchase commodities. How does the reality fit the model? How many people actually calculate the utility for a given expenditure when they make a purchasing decision? Most consumers have never consciously computed any utility that determines their satisfaction for a given budget, but consumers are making "rational decisions" directly based on their satisfaction or intuition -- that is, what they like and do not like. Consumers often make purchasing and consumption decisions based on their intuition and on their feelings.

SOURCES OF CONSUMER SATISFACTION

Consumers' satisfaction comes not only from the product itself but also from the packaging, advertising, sales environment, after-sale services, and warranties.

For instance, a piece of clothing can provide satisfaction, even if the consumer does not wear it. Lisa has a large variety of clothes at her home. When she wanders about at a shopping mall, she sees a beautiful piece of clothing. She purchases the clothing, puts it into her closet, and hopes someday she can wear it. Years pass, but she has not had a chance to wear that piece of clothing. One day her family moves. As she cleans her closet, she decides the piece of clothing is no longer needed, and she finally throws away the clothing as trash. Did Lisa make a rational decision when she purchased that item?

The answer is "Yes, she made a "rational decision" in terms of satisfying herself." The answer is "No, if we consider how Lisa reached her decision. She did not calculate utility, nor did she go through a mathematical and rational decision-making process."

Consider the "rational" aspect of her decision-making. What satisfied her was not actually wearing the clothing day in and day out. It was the enjoyment she got when she purchased the clothing, kept the clothing in her closet, and showed it to her friends. *Consumer utility maximization* is to maximize the satisfaction and the feeling of being satisfied. It is not about whether the goods perform the functions for which they are technically designed and manufactured. The function and performance of merchandise are just two of many ways it can satisfy a consumer.

Goods produce enjoyment and satisfaction not only from final consumption but also from window-shopping, purchasing, and possession. Goods can produce consumer satisfaction even before they are sold. This is what people call window-shopping.

When we consider Lisa's "irrational" decision-making behavior, we may be tempted to encourage consumers like Lisa to use "rational decision-making process" based on advanced economic and mathematical knowledge. When we try to apply a rational decision-making process into the real world circumstance, we will find maximizing utility with 100% certainty is almost impossible, and rational decision-making is not without cost.

UTILITY MAXIMIZATION CANNOT BE ACHIEVED WITH 100% CERTAINTY

On average, consumers are trying to maximize their satisfaction. This is the rational side of decision-making. However, in the real world, consumers may not reach their maximum satisfaction due to a variety of reasons, such as the cost of decision-making, time constraint, and insufficient information. Consumers' desires to make rational decisions are restricted by real world conditions. For example, the Wang family plans a vacation to Asia from the U.S. The objective is to achieve the lowest airfare. There are hundreds of travel agents, and many airlines. Mr. Wang calls several travel agencies and purchases the tickets from one of them. When the family returns from traveling, a friend tells them that if they had purchased the tickets from ZYX Travel Agency, they would have saved several hundred dollars. This case illustrates the fact that although average consumers are trying to maximize their satisfaction, the reality is that consumers cannot reach the theoretical maximum utility point. The theoretical consumer behavior model does not take into consideration factors such as the cost of collecting information, the cost of purchasing,

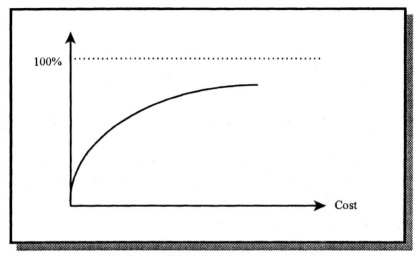

Figure 4.1   The Probability of Making A Correct Decision

the cost incurred in decision-making, and the time spent in decision-making. What the average consumers can achieve is the practical optimal satisfaction level given the cost of decision-making. It appears that average consumers are not reaching the maximum level of utility (satisfaction) when they make "rational decisions."

Rational decision-making can be extremely difficult, as the following story illustrates. In Figure 4.1, the vertical axis is the probability in percentage that the purchasing decision will be the correct decision. The horizontal axis is the cost, including money spent for decision-making, money spent for collecting information, time, etc. The higher the cost, the higher the chance the purchasing decision will be correct.

For example, Mr. Johnson wants to purchase a used car. He first purchases a used-car buyer guide. It takes him 4 hours to find this book in the bookstore. It costs him $5.00. When he finds a car he would like to purchase, he is not sure the car is in good mechanical condition. He sends the car to a garage for an $80 checkup. When he finally chooses a car to purchase, he has already spent 20 hours driving around to check out different cars. So his total cost will be $85 ($80 + $5) and 24 hours (20 hours + 4 hours). Generally speaking, the more time and money he spent on the decision-making, the higher the chance the decision will be correct. In addition to this, Mr. Johnson rented a car to use before he got his own

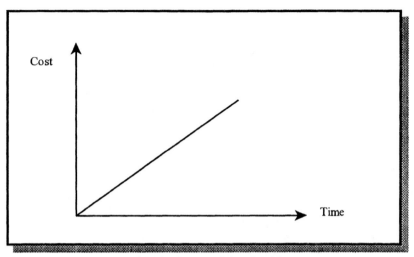

Figure 4.2   Cost of Delaying Decision Making

car. The more time it takes to purchase a car, the more the car-rental fee becomes. He also lost wages since he needed the time to look for a car. The more time he uses to search for the right car, the more wages he loses. This kind of cost is often directly correlated with the time needed to make a decision. This is illustrated in Figure 4.2.

Consumer decision-making is a complex process if it is to be done by logical reasoning. Therefore, consumers, although trying to maximize their utility, will never be able to achieve utility maximization 100% of the time. There is always room for improvement.

Business and government decisions are very similar, particularly when it comes to what projects to undertake, and what equipment to purchase. For example, after years of study on the Three Gorge Project, China decided in the 1990s to go ahead with it. After the project started, some brilliant engineers suggested that the same set of objectives could be achieved if several smaller dams were built instead of one large dam. This option suggested that the cost and risk could both be cut. However, it was already too late. (It is still debatable which option is the best). Figure 4.1 and Figure 4.2 also apply to business and government decision-making. The net benefit of decision-making can be illustrated by Figure 4.3. The vertical is the net benefit in a statistical sense; the horizontal is the time and money used for decision-making. In principle, we know the net benefit of

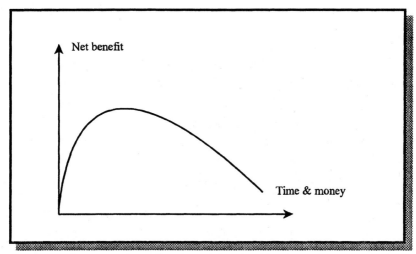

Figure 4.3   Net Benefit of Decision-Making

decision-making increases up to a particular point as more time and money are spent on that decision-making; after reaching the peak point, the net benefit of decision-making decreases, as more time and money are spent on decision-making results in less marginal return. In reality, it is much harder, if not impossible, to figure out how much decision-making is optimal.

SUMMARY OF UTILITY MAXIMIZATION

From the above discussion, we can conclude that the consumption decisions made by a business, a government or an individual follow a statistical pattern. The maximum net benefit of decision-making is achieved when the time and money spent on decision-making are at a proper level. Above or below such a level, the net benefit of decision-making will decrease in a statistical sense. However, finding such a proper level of decision-making is extremely difficult, if not impossible. The utility maximization for an individual, business, or a government cannot be achieved with 100% certainty.

THE ERROR IN MARGINALIST VALUE THEORY

Mainstream economists believe that as a result of utility maximization, the following equation holds true:

$$MU = P$$

Where:

       MU: marginal utility
       P: price

In the following discussion argues that the MU does not equal price when consumers maximize their total utility.

Suppose Mr. Jevons has a given consumption budget. He has two goods to choose from -- lemons and pineapples. His utility indifference

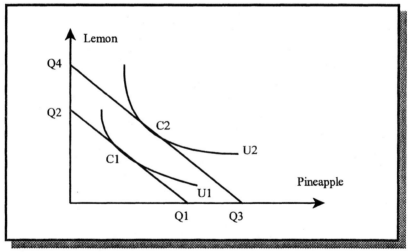

Figure 4.4   Utility Level Under Different Budgets

curves and budget constraint are shown in Figure 4.4. Assume the prices of lemons and pineapples do not change.

First, we give Mr. Jevons a budget constraint, which is presented as a straight line Q1 to Q2. Mr. Jevons' utility indifference curve U1, is tangent to this budget constraint (purchasing possibility curve) at point C1. At C1, Mr. Jevons maximizes his total utility within the given budget constraint curve, as defined by a straight line connecting Q1 and Q2.

Second, when we give more money to Mr. Jevons to spend, his budget constraint line shifts to the right. The new budget constraint line is the straight line connecting points Q3 and Q4. His new utility indifference curve, U2, is tangent to the new budget constraint line at point C2.

Mr. Jevons consumes more pineapples and lemons at point C2 than at point C1. According to the diminishing marginal utility (refer to Chapter 2), the marginal utility for pineapples at C2 is lower than the marginal utility for pineapples at C1. Similarly, the marginal utility for lemons at C2 is lower than the marginal utility for lemons at C1. This can be expressed with the following formula:

MU2 (pineapples) < MU1 (pineapples)
MU2 (lemons) < MU1 (lemons)

Where:

MU2 (pineapples): marginal utility at C2 for the last pineapple
MU1 (pineapples): marginal utility at C1 for the last pineapple
MU2 (lemons):   marginal utility at C2 for the last lemon
MU1 (lemons):   marginal utility at C1 for the last lemon

Because the price of pineapples has not changed while the budget constraint line shifts, it is not possible to have the following two equations both be true, since MU2 (pineapples) < MU1 (pineapples).

MU2 (pineapples) = price of pineapples
MU1 (pineapples) = price of pineapples

The above equations suggest that MU2 (pineapples) = MU1 (pineapples), which as we have shown in the above discussion, are not equal due to diminishing marginal utility. Therefore, marginal utility cannot be equal to the price, as mainstream economics claims.

Because the price of the lemons has not changed while the budget constraint line shifts, it is not possible to have the following two equations both be true, since MU2 (lemons) < MU1 (lemons). According to MU=P, we have the following two equations.

MU2 (lemons) = price of lemons
MU1 (lemons) = price of lemons

The above two equations suggest that MU2 (lemons) = MU1 (lemons), which as we have shown in above discussion, are not equal due to diminishing marginal utility. Therefore, we have shown that the marginal utility is not equal to the price of the goods.

The reason marginal utility is not equal to price is because of the budget constraint. The mainstream theory of exchange value may hold true if consumers, business purchasers, and government agencies are not subject to spending limits and budget constraints. However, as we know in the real world, no one can escape spending limits. This is illustrated in Figure 4.5.

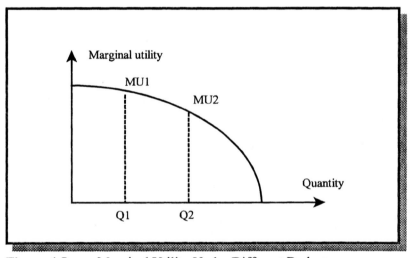

Figure 4.5   Marginal Utility Under Different Budgets

Figure 4.5 illustrates a single commodity model for the diminishing marginal utility. The vertical axis is the marginal utility level for each additional commodity consumed. The horizontal axis represents the total quantity consumed. The utility curve goes down as more commodities are consumed; meanwhile, marginal utility diminishes as each additional commodity is added into consumption.

Suppose the commodity is turkey meat. Suppose the price of the turkey is $4 per kilogram. The budget is $20. The consumer can consume a total of 5 kilograms of turkey ($20/$4 = 5). Let Q1 = 5 kilograms of turkey. The marginal utility of the turkey is MU1. MU1 is the marginal utility point that corresponds to Q1. If we give the consumer more money to spend, he will be able to purchase more turkey. Suppose we increase his budget to $40. He can purchase 10 kilograms of turkey. Let Q2 = 10 kilograms of turkey. MU2 is the marginal utility for the consumption level of Q2. As we see in Figure 4.5, MU2 < MU1 due to the diminishing marginal utility. The marginal utility may be denoted by a monetary unit; for example, we can assume that MU1 = P = $4.00. Clearly, we are not able to make both MU1 and MU2 equal to the same price. Therefore, the equation MU = P is wrong.

In conclusion, marginal utility does not equal price. The mainstream value theory is incorrect. The marginal utility theory, therefore, cannot explain the exchange value.

INTRODUCTION TO PRICE THEORY

In an ideal economy, when the economy is operating at its peak efficiency, the major economic parameters have a special relationship as shown in the following equation.

$$R + 1 = L + 1 = P + 1 = (C + 1)(1 + B) = (1 + S)(1 + I)$$

Where:

C: price change rate for the product
S: productivity growth rate of an economy
B: productivity growth rate of a business, or an industry
I: inflation rate of the economy
L: labor monetary compensation increase rate
R: interest rate
P: profit rate

We obtain this result by applying the equal exchange of value to the economy. In other words, if the market can automatically apply the rule of equal exchange to all transactions in the market, the major economic parameters will have the above relations. If the major economic parameters of an economy have the above relations, the economy will operate at its peak efficiency.

In Chapter Three, we discovered the optimal parameters for the real economy. This is the Law of Optimal Parameters for the Real World Economy.

$$V(1) = V(0)[(1 + S)(1 + I) - \Delta$$
$$(1 + C)(1 + B) = (1 + S)(1 + I) - \Delta$$
$$1 + R = (1 + S)(1 + I) - \Delta$$
$$1 + P = (1 + S)(1 + I) - \Delta$$
$$1 + L = (1 + S)(1 + I) - \Delta$$

Where:

Δ:	wage compensator
C:	price change rate for the product
S:	productivity growth rate of a economy
B:	productivity growth rate of a business or an industry
I:	inflation rate of the economy (consumer goods and services)
L:	labor monetary compensation increase rate
R:	interest rate (nominal interest rate)
P:	profit rate of a business or industry, or the average profit rate of the economy (nominal profit rate)
V(1):	monetary equivalent of one labor hour at the end of the period
V(0):	monetary equivalent of one labor hour at the beginning of the period

In this section, we will study price theory, the theory of nominal interest rate, and the theory of nominal profit rate. We will try to answer the following questions: How does the market mechanism work in terms of applying the rule of equal exchange of value? When does the market work by the rule of equal exchange of value? When will it not work? We will try to compare the price movement, interest rate, and profit rate with the optimal parameters shown in the above equations.

THEORY OF PRICE

The theory of price is the study of price movement. Price is determined by the supply curve and the demand curve. Therefore, the theory of price studies the factors that affect or determine supply and demand.

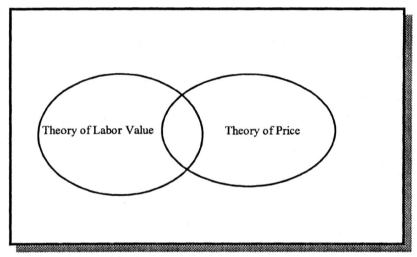

Figure 4.6   Domains

BETWEEN THEORY OF VALUE AND THEORY OF PRICE

The theory of price is different from the theory of value. The theory of value studies the average price movement, and what determines it. What we have studied in the first, second, and third chapters is the theory of value. The theory of price studies the factors that will affect and determine the actual price, not the average price. The theory of price and the theory of value have different domains. The domain defines the area to which the theory can be applied. A theory is only valid in its defined domain. The theory of value studied in this book is specifically called the labor theory of value. We have proved that the theory of value based on marginal utility is wrong. Figure 4.6 shows the relationship between the domains of the theory of labor value and the theory of price.

In some situations, the labor theory of value does not apply. For example, the labor theory of value is only intended to explain the average price for reproducible goods. Therefore, if we are discussing a commodity that is not reproducible, then the labor theory of value may not apply. While the theory of price can explain more things, it, too, has limitations. The theory of price cannot explain   long-run equilibrium, or optimal economic parameters.

THE SUPPLY AND DEMAND CURVE

The market works magically to achieve equal exchange of value without government intervention for most commodities. The supply and demand at the marketplace determine the price of the commodity. When the

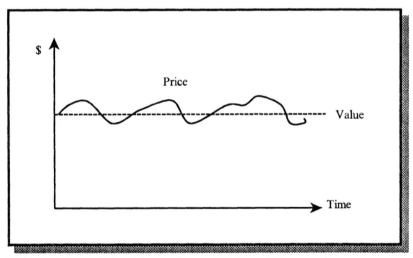

Figure 4.7   Price Moves Around Value of Commodity

price is higher than the labor value of the commodity, more commodities will be produced since it becomes more profitable to produce more. This requires that the goods be reproducible and that the market be perfectly competitive. The buyers will purchase less when the price is high. This will drive the price of the goods down toward the labor value of the commodity. When the price of the commodity is lower than the labor value of the commodity, the supply will decrease, because it becomes less profitable to produce more. Producers will reduce production. This situation may force some corporations out of business. The buyers will purchase more as the price is lower. This drives the price of the commodity higher toward the labor value of the commodity. The market achieves equal exchange value by frequently deviating from the labor value. The price deviation from the labor value of the commodity signals the buyer and the producer as to what to do. Therefore, on average, the market achieves equal exchange of value. Figure 4.7 illustrates price movement around the value of the commodity.

The price is determined by the supply curve and the demand curve, as is shown in Figure 4.8.

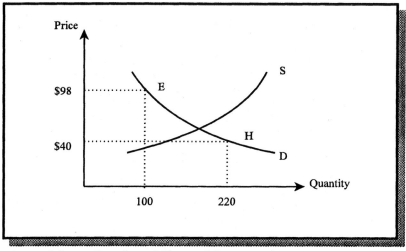

Figure 4.8   Supply and Demand Curve

The demand curve presents the relations between price and quantity demanded. In Figure 4.8, D curve is the demand curve, and S is the supply curve. Point H on the demand curve in Figure 4.8 corresponds to quantity 220, and price $40. Point E is a point on the demand curve D in Figure 4.8, which shows when the price is $98, the quantity demanded is 100. The lower the price, the higher the quantity demanded. The price is lower at point H than point E. Quantity demanded increases from 100 at point E, to 220 at point H. Similarly, the supply curve presents the relations between price and quantity supplied. The higher the price, the higher the quantity supplied. There are many factors that affect the demand curve. Similarly, there are many factors that affect the supply curve. I will give a brief discussion here because they have been studied in detail in mainstream economic textbooks (Refer to any microeconomic textbook for detail). Supply and demand curves describe the price and quantity relation for a given duration. When the duration changes, the supply and demand curve will also change.

Demand curve may be affected by the following factors: the income (budget constraint), time, substitute effect, complementary effect, and change in demand. An increase in income will shift the demand curve to the right. This means that at the same price level, consumers will consume more of the goods.

For example, as people make more money, they will spend more on vacation, purchase more new homes, buy more new automobiles, and dine out more often at restaurants. If we compare people with different levels of income, we will find that richer people have more vacations, bigger houses, more automobiles, and they eat out more often at a restaurant. This is the income effect.

It takes time for consumers to notice the price change, and it takes time for consumers to respond to a change in price. The longer the duration, the flatter the demand curve will become. For short time duration, the demand curve tends to be steeper. This is the time or duration effect.

When one commodity can be substituted for another, the two commodities will have what is called a substitute effect. For example, Mr. James has two options to get to work daily. One is to drive his car to his office in New York; the other is to take a train. As the cost of driving to work increases, he would be more likely to take the train. If the cost of taking the train increases dramatically relative to the cost of driving by himself, he would be more likely to switch to driving. The demand curve for the train is affected by the total cost of driving. As driving cost increases, the demand for a train ride will also increase. This is the substitute effect.

Products that are usually consumed together are complementary products. For example, a personal computer and the monitor, a printer and printer paper. A decrease in the price of the printer will increase the consumption of both printer and printer paper. Similarly, a decrease in the price of personal computers will increase the sale of monitors. This is the complementary effect.

There are many other factors that can result in a change in demand. For example, when natural disasters such as mud slides, and earthquakes happen, the demands for first aid and emergency commodities increase. This causes a shift in the demand curve. On days of heavy rain, the demand for umbrellas increases, and stores will sell more umbrellas than on normal days. This is called a shift (change) in demand.

The supply curve is affected by many factors, such as economic scale, diminishing marginal return, and monopoly. The economic scale refers to the decrease in average cost, when there is any increase in the production volume. In other words, the productivity increases as the production output volume increases. Economic scale produces a supply curve such that as quantity increases, price decreases.

Diminishing marginal return happens when we increase one production factor to a certain point while holding other input factors constant. For example, for a given acreage of farm land, if we keep adding labor force to the land, the output of the crop will at first increase. When the output of the crop reaches a certain point, additional labor force would do less good. The productivity of the additional labor decreases, and the additional output each additional laborer brings decreases. When the diminishing marginal return happens, the slope of the supply curve tends to increase. Monopoly brings a lower quantity of products to the market; it also causes price level increases. This is equivalent to shifting the supply curve to the left.

In the following I will combine knowledge about the labor theory of value and the theory of price to explain price movement processes in two simple models with a shift of demand curve. They are simple models because they are simplified by these following assumptions: (1) no productivity improvement of the product in concern, (2) a perfect competitive market, and (3) no inflation. In the first case, the demand curve shifts to the right; and in the second case, the demand curve shifts to the left.

WHEN DEMAND CURVE SHIFTS TO THE RIGHT

In the short run, the supply curve will respond to the price change by a change in the quantity supplied. Nevertheless, in the long run the supply curve is determined by the labor value needed to reproduce the commodity. If there is no inflation, no productivity improvement of the economy, and no productivity improvement related to the commodity, the average price of the commodity will remain the same in the long run. We can obtain this by using the following equation (Chapter 3):

$$(1 + C)(1 + B) = (1 + S)(1 + I) - \Delta$$

When:

$B = I = S = 0$

$C = - \Delta$

When $\Delta = 0$, $C = 0$

Because Δ is often a very small number, we ignore it in the following analysis.

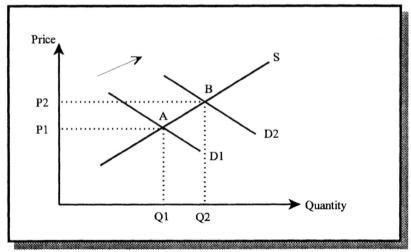

Figure 4.9   Shift of Demand Curve to the Right

I will now show what happens in the process when there is a shift in the demand curve. In Figure 4.9, there is a supply curve S and two demand curves D1 and D2. Assume at the beginning the demand curve was D1. It then shifts to the right. This is denoted by D2. The quantity of consumption increases from Q1 to Q2. The price of the commodity also increases from P1 to P2. This is because in the short run, producers will respond to an increase in demand by increasing prices. As the price is higher, more profit is generated. Producers will produce more products in pursuit of profit in a perfect competitive market.

As more products make it to the market, the price of the product will fall back to the level determined by the socially necessary labor needed to reproduce the goods. This is illustrated by Figure 4.10.

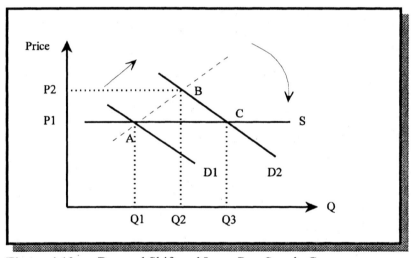

Figure 4.10   Demand Shift and Long-Run Supply Curve

When the price level returns to the original level, which is the price level that correctly reflects the labor value necessary to reproduce the commodity, the long run supply curve is flat because there is neither productivity improvement nor inflation. We can obtain this by applying the equation developed in Chapter 2. The quantity consumed increases again from Q2 to Q3. The price level drops from P2 to P1. In the long run, the shift in a demand curve will move the consumption from point A to point

B, then to point C. During this process, the price level first goes up and then comes down to where it started. It is illustrated by Figure 4.11.

In Figure 4.11, the horizontal is the time line. The vertical is the price level. The straight flat line v (price = P1) is the price level that reflects the value of the commodity. At T1, the demand curve is D1 as it is in Figures 4.9 and 4.10. As the demand curve shifts to D2 in Figure 4.9,

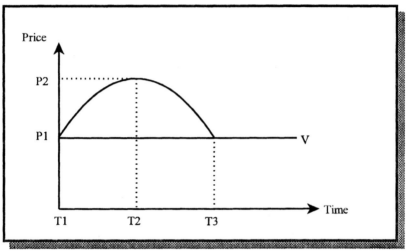

Figure 4.11   Price Change Over Time

the price increases to P2. It corresponds to time T2. When the supply curve starts to react to the shift of the demand curve, the price level drops to P1 at time T3. We also observe that the quantity of consumption increases from point A to point B, and from B to C in Figure 4.10. In other words, the consumption increases from T1 to T2, and also increases from T2 to T3. This can be illustrated by Figure 4.12. The time interval from T1 to T2 may not equal the time interval from T2 to T3. The consumption quantity increases from Q1 to Q2 may not be the same as from Q2 to Q3, even though a straight line in Figure 4.12 may suggest that they are equal.

In Figure 4.12, the horizontal axis is still the time line. The vertical axis is the consumption level. It increases from Q1 to Q2, then to Q3. From this process, during which we assume that there is no productivity improvement of the product or economy and that there is no inflation, we

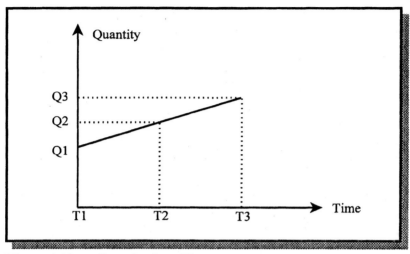

Figure 4.12   Quantity Over Time

can conclude the following:

1.   The supply curve moves as our observation changes from the short-term to the long-term. The slope of the supply curve reduces to zero from a positive number as we move from the short-run to the long-run.
2.   The supply curve will react to the change in the demand curve. A change in demand will trigger a reaction from the supply curve.
3.   Consumption increases as the price increases during the period from T1 to T2. This is caused by the shift of the demand curve.
4.   If we observe the price of a commodity change with an increase-decrease pattern as shown in Figure 4.11, we know that there is a shift of the demand curve to the right. It suggests an increase in the quantity consumed.

WHEN DEMAND CURVE SHIFTS TO THE LEFT

In the short run, the supply curve will respond to the price change by a change in the quantity supplied. However, in the long run the supply curve is determined by the labor value needed to reproduce the commodity. We can obtain this by using the following equation (Chapter 3):

$$(1 + C)(1 + B) = (1 + S)(1 + I) - \Delta$$

When:
$$B = I = S = 0$$
$$C = - \Delta$$
When $\Delta = 0$, $C = 0$

Because Δ is often a very small number, we ignore it in the following analysis.

Now, I will show what happens in the process, when there is a shift to the left in the demand curve. Figure 4.13 presents a supply curve S and two demand curves D1 and D2. Assume that at the beginning, the demand curve was D1. It then shifts to the left, denoted by D2. The quantity of consumption decreases from Q1 to Q2. The price of the commodity also decreases from P1 to P2. This is because in the short run, producers will respond to the decrease in demand by reducing prices. As the price is lower, less profit is generated. Producers will produce fewer products to reduce loss in a perfect competitive market.

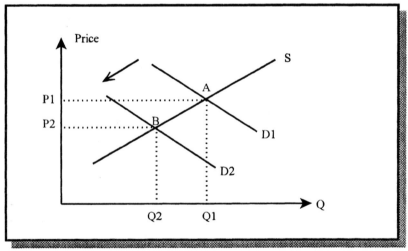

Figure 4.13   Demand Curve Shifts to the Left

As fewer products make it to the market, the price of the product will go up to the level determined by the socially necessary labor needed to produce the goods. This is illustrated by Figure 4.14.

When the price level returns to the original level, we assume that it is equivalent to the labor value necessary to reproduce the commodity.

The quantity consumed decreases again from Q2 to Q3, while the price level moves up from P2 to P1. In the long run, the shift in a demand curve will move the consumption from point A to B, then back to C. During this process, the price level first goes down to P2, then gets back to where it started. This change is illustrated by Figure 4.14.

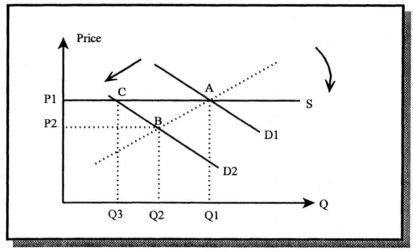

Figure 4.14   Demand Curve Shift in Long-Run Supply Curve

In Figure 4.15, the horizontal axis is the time line. The vertical is the price level. The straight flat line V (Price = P1) is the price level that reflects the value of the commodity. At T1, the demand curve is D1 as it is in Figure 4.13. As the demand curve shifts to D2 in Figure 4.13, the price decreases to P2. It corresponds to time T2. When the supply curve starts to react to the shift of demand curve, the price level increases to P1 point C as in Figure 4.14 and T3 as in Figure 4.15. We also observe the quantity of consumption decreases from point A to B, and from B to C in Figure 4.14. In other words, the consumption decreases from T1 to T2, and also decreases from T2 to T3. This can be illustrated by Figure 4.16.

In Figure 4.16, the horizontal axis is still the time line. The vertical axis is the consumption level. It decreases from Q1 to Q2, then to Q3.

From this process, we can conclude the following:

1.   The supply curve moves as our observation changes from short-term to long-term. The slope of the supply curve reduces to zero

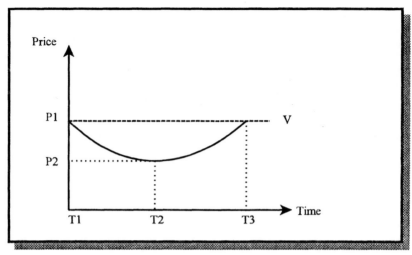

Figure 4.15   Price Change Over Time

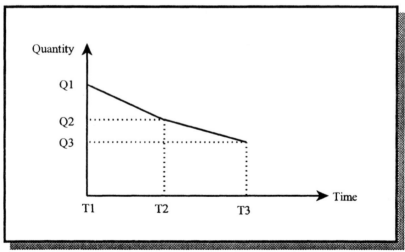

Figure 4.16   Quantity Change Over Time

from a positive number as we move from the short-run to the long-run.

2.   The supply curve will react to the change of demand curve. A change in demand will trigger a reaction from the supply curve.

3.   The consumption decreases as the price decreases during the period from T1 to T2. This is caused by the shift of the demand curve to the left. The consumption continues to decrease from T2 to T3 in Figure 4.15 as the price level goes back to P1.

Combining information illustrated in Figure 4.11 and 4.15, we get a complete picture of a typical cycle of price movement. It is illustrated in Figure 4.17.

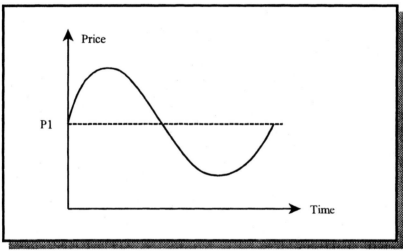

Figure 4.17   Price Cycle Over Time

APPLICATION

EXAMPLE 4.1

If we know the slope of the demand curve, we can estimate the quantity change. For example, suppose we know the demand curve has a slope of -0.8 where the quantity is in thousands, and the price is in dollars. The slope of the demand curve is defined as below.

slope = change in price/change in quantity

(Refer to Figure 4.14.) Assume that Q2 = 100 thousand units, P1 = $12, and P2 = $8. We are to estimate the quantity of Q3.

slope = - 0.8 = change in price/change in quantity
slope = (8 -12)/(Q2 - Q3) =-4/(100 - Q3)
- 0.8 × (100 - Q3) = - 4
(100 - Q3) = 4/0.8 = 5
100 - 5 = Q3 = 95 thousand units

In the above analysis, we simplify the model by making the following assumptions: (1) no productivity improvement of the product concerned ; (2) a perfect competitive market; (3) no inflation; and (4) no productivity improvement in the economy as a whole. Additional models can be built to study what happens when these assumptions are removed.

SHIFT OF THE SUPPLY CURVE

Next, we will study the shift of the supply curve with both the knowledge of the labor theory of value and the theory of price by examining one simple model. It is a simple model because it is simplified by the following assumptions: (1) no change in the demand curve; and (2) a perfect competitive market.

Use this equation from Chapter 3:
$(1 + C)(1 + B) = (1 + S)(1 + I) - \Delta$

In Figure 4.18, there is a demand curve D with slope β. It is not going to shift or change during the analysis. There are two long-run supply curves. Because it is a long-run supply curve, it is flat and determined by the labor value necessary to produce the commodity. When there is a productivity improvement, the long-run supply curve shifts downward, from S1 to S2. Before the productivity improvement, the quantity consumed is at Q1 with price P1. After the productivity improvement, the quantity consumed increases to Q2 while the price reduces to P2.

$\beta = (P2 - P1)/(Q2 - Q1)$

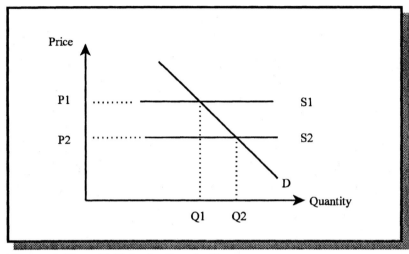

Figure 4.18   Shift in the Supply Curve

In an ideal economy, the percentage price change for a product is C.

$$C = (P2 - P1)/P1$$

When C < 0, there is a price reduction. When C > 0, there is a rise in price. Therefore,

$$\beta = (C \times P1)/(Q2 - Q1)$$
$$(1 + C)(1 + B) = (1 + S)(1 + I) - \Delta$$

Where:

C:	price change rate for the product
S:	productivity growth rate of the economy
B:	productivity growth rate of the business or the industry
β:	slope of the demand curve
I:	inflation rate

When we combine the above two equations, we can solve for two unknown variables.

EXAMPLE 4.2

Assume that $\beta = -0.8$ (price in dollars, quantity in million units). $Q1 = 2$ million units. $P1 = \$89$, $B = 30\%$, $S = 2.5\%$, $I = 0\%$, $\Delta = 0$

$$-0.8 = C \times 89/(Q2 - 2)$$
$$(C + 1)(1 + 0.3) = (1 + 0.025)$$

we have:

$$C = -0.2116$$
$$Q2 = 23.53 \text{ million units}$$

The result shows that the price will decrease by about 21%, and the quantity of commodity consumed will increase to about 24 million units from 2 million. When the economy has a 2.5% productivity improvement, the business has a 30% productivity improvement, initial price is \$89, and demand curve slope is -0.8.

EXAMPLE 4.3

Suppose for color TVs, we have the following observations: $\beta = -1.4$, $P1 = \$300$, $Q2 - Q1 = 21$ million units, $S = 7\%$. The currency unit is dollars, and the quantity is in million units. We are to solve for B and S, while $I = 0$ and $\Delta = 0$.

$$\beta = CP1/(Q2 - Q1)$$
$$(1 + C)(1 + B) = (1 + S)(1 + I) - \Delta$$

$$-1.4 = (\$300 \times C)/21$$
$$(1 + C)(1 + B) = (1 + 7\%)$$

$$C = -9.8\%$$
$$B = 18.6\%$$

The results are a 9.8% decrease in price, and a 18.6% increase in the productivity of TV manufacturing. When the demand slope is -1.4, initial price of the TV is \$300.00, quantity sold increases 21 millions, and the economy has a 7% productivity growth rate for the same period.

THE DIFFERENCE BETWEEN THE PERFECT COMPETITIVE MARKET AND THE IDEAL ECONOMY

In the first chapter, we discussed the perfect competitive market and its characteristics. The ideal economy must also be a perfect competitive market. The perfect market may or may not be an ideal economy. In an ideal economy the following relationships exist between major economic parameters.

$$R + 1 = L + 1 = P + 1 = (C + 1)(1 + B) = (1 + S)(1 + I)$$

In a perfect competitive market, these relationships may not exist. We can use these equations in the perfect competitive market because we assume that the perfect competitive market is very close to the ideal economy. How close the real world economy is to the ideal economy, what makes the real world economy move toward the ideal economy, and what makes the real world economy move away from the ideal economy are the subjects we will investigate in this chapter.

THE THEORY OF NOMINAL INTEREST RATE AND NOMINAL PROFIT RATE

DEFINITION AND CONCEPT

Chapter One and Chapter Two studied the average interest rate in the perfect competitive market and in an ideal market respectively. Nominal interest rate is not the average interest rate – simply the actual market interest rate. In the theory of nominal interest rate, we will study all the factors that can change the rate of interest. Nominal profit rate is not the average profit rate; it is the actual profit rate in the marketplace. In the theory of nominal profit rate, we will study all the factors that can change the rate of profit. Similarly, we will study the forces that move the profit rate.

When there is 10% inflation, and a saving account earns a 10% interest rate, the saving account does not actually earn anything real, since inflation devalues the money. On average, the purchasing power of the money does not change. Therefore, the real interest rate here is zero. Putting it into an equation, we define the real interest rate as follows:

real interest rate = nominal interest rate - inflation rate

A similar situation exists for the return on stocks. When there is 10% inflation, and a stock earns a 10% profit rate, the stock investment does not actually earn anything real, since inflation devalues the money. On average, the purchasing power does not change. Therefore, the return on stocks, the real profit rate in this case, is zero. Putting it into an equation, we define the real profit rate as follows:

real profit rate = nominal profit rate - inflation rate
When inflation rate = 0
real profit rate = nominal profit rate

Table 4.1 illustrates hypothetical average nominal profit rates for companies listed on a stock market during the years 1994 to 1999.

Table 4.1

Year	1994	1995	1996	1997	1998	1999
Nominal profit rate	34%	26%	27%	24%	10%	8%

By simply looking at this data, investors could complain that the business performance has declined over time. However the business performance may actually have increased during this period of time if inflation is taken into consideration. Table 4.2 includes the inflation and real profit rate. The real profit rate shows that the business performance is not getting worse over time. The worse year was actually 1995, not 1999.

Therefore, business people and economists should look at the real profit rate instead of the nominal profit rate when evaluating a business performance. Often, the nominal profit rate in isolation can be very misleading.

Table 4.2

Year	1994	1995	1996	1997	1998	1999
Nominal profit rate	34%	26%	27%	24%	10%	8%
Inflation rate	25%	21%	15%	11%	-1%	-3%
Real profit rate	9%	5%	12%	13%	11%	11%

THE THEORY OF NOMINAL INTEREST RATE AND NOMINAL PROFIT RATE

The nominal interest rate is determined by the supply and demand for money. Figure 4.19 illustrates the supply and demand curve for money at different interest rates. The vertical axis is the nominal interest rate. To the money borrower, the interest rate determines the cost of borrowing money. To the money lender, the interest rate is the return on the investment. First, look at the supply curve. The supply of money comes from people's savings. The S curve is the supply curve; and the D curve is the demand curve for money.

THE SUPPLY CURVE OF MONEY

Consumer income is either used for consumption or savings. So we have:

income = consumption + savings

savings = income - consumption

Consumption refers to consumer goods purchased, such as housing, transportation, education, clothing, food, and entertainment.

Savings is money put aside for investment, or kept in a bank account. People usually save money for a purpose. That is for future consumption or investment, such as to purchase a car, to buy a house, to retire, to take a vacation, to get a university education, or to start a new business. When people decide to save money, they rarely change the amount saved even if there is a change in the interest rate. Therefore, the supply curve is very close to a vertical curve within a certain interest rate

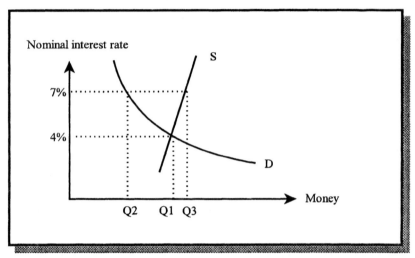

Figure 4.19   Supply and Demand for Money–Capital

range. For example, in China, consumer savings increased from 1997 to 1999, while at the same time the bank interest rate decreased from about 10% to 3%. Although savings rate has a lot to do with culture and traditions, as well as economic factors, it is difficult to believe that people will save more if an interest rate is higher. Do people cut their mortgage payment, or expenditures on clothes, transportation costs, or vacations, simply because the bank interest rate goes up by 2 percentage points? Probably not. However, every time the bank increases its interest rate, it does so hoping to attract more savings. Although total savings are less sensitive to the interest rate, consumers can move their investment from stocks to interest-bearing securities as the interest rate goes up, and vice versa. Banks may attract more money when the interest rate is up, but this may not be the result of increased savings and investments from consumers.

In a globalized economy, when banks in Hong Kong increase their interest rate relative to the banks in Japan, people in Japan will move their savings into banks in Hong Kong that have the higher interest rate, assuming that their exchange rate does not change. Although the banks in Hong Kong increase their money by attracting more money, the interest rate does little to change people's decisions to save or to consume. The money Hong Kong attracts is from Japan. And the money is designated by Japanese consumers as savings and investment regardless of whether or not Hong Kong has increased its interest rate. What usually changes consumers' saving and consumption behavior is their income level today and expected income in the near future. This has a lot to do with the general economic confidence of consumers.

Another major factor that influences consumers' saving behavior is inflation and expected return on consumer goods purchased. Here the distinction between investment and consumption becomes blurred. When consumers find they can make more money by purchasing a commodity such as a house or car and later selling it at a higher price, they will purchase those goods for both consumption and investment. This kind of situation happens in inflation, especially when inflation is higher than the productivity growth rate of the economy.

However, a lower interest rate does have a dramatic effect on consumption financing. For example, as the interest rate decreases, housing construction and new home sales go up. Overall, the supply curve tends to be quite vertical.

For most investment vehicles today, liquidity is not a major problem. A rational consumer will maximize his or her return on the money for investment instead of being concerned with liquidity. For example, investors can get their mutual-fund money back in one or two weeks. If investors sell their stocks, the money from the selling of the stock usually becomes available to the investors in two or three days. Some investment firms offer customers checking accounts on their investment funds. Some stocks and some mutual funds have become as liquid as a checking account in a local bank.

EQUALIZATION OF MARGINAL RETURN ON INVESTMENT

Let us consider an example here. Mr. Chen may have the following choices for his money: a bank saving account, a Certificate of Deposit, corporate bonds, government bonds, and stocks. As a rational investor, he will maximize total return - expected value. Suppose Mr. Chen is concerned only with investing for a one-year period. He estimates the stock has the following expected returns at different levels of probability taking into consideration the transaction cost and management cost of his stock accounts (Table 4.3):

Table 4.3

Probability	5%	70%	15%	10%
Rate of return	22%	8%	5%	-30%

The expected return of the stock investment is:

$$E(S) = 22\% \times 5\% + 8\% \times 70\% + 5\% \times 15\% + (-30\%) \times 10\%$$
$$= 4.45\%$$

Mr. Chen will estimate all the other investment vehicles and decide to invest his money in the one that has the highest expected return. As every investor seeks maximization of returns on investment at the capital (investment) market, all the different investment vehicles will be forced to equalize on expected marginal return on investment. Expected return on all investments will be equalized at equilibrium. As more money is poured into the investment vehicle that has the highest expected marginal return, the expected marginal return of the investment vehicle will decrease as more money is invested in it. Eventually all investment options should have the same marginal returns.

When there is no government control of interest rates and intervention, the market balances its marginal return on investments. For example, if the corporate profit growth rate is up, the stock market is up. More investment money will be moved from other investment vehicles to stock until the marginal returns on all investment vehicles are equal. When there is an increase in government debts, the government will issue government bonds to pay for the debts. The interest on the government bonds must be high enough to attract investment from other securities into government bonds. The result is the same; the marginal return on all investments must be equalized at equilibrium.

When there is government intervention in the securities market or in control of the lending interest rate, the situation is slightly different. When a government's central bank reduces the interest rate relative to the marginal return on stocks, the stock market will go up. More investment money will be moved to the stock market until the expected marginal return on stocks is equal to the prevalent interest rate. When the government increases the interest rate relative to the marginal return on stocks, the money will be attracted from stock investments to interest-bearing securities.

THE DEMAND CURVE FOR MONEY

The demand for money (capital) depends on the ability of business people and governments to find projects that can generate expected returns higher than the cost of borrowing -- the interest rate. The projects can be anything, such as an airport, a highway, a bridge, a manufacturing facility, a hotel, an apartment complex, a housing development project, a ship, or a university. The lower the interest, the higher the number of projects that will become profitable, and the more capital that will be demanded. Therefore, we have the demand curves illustrated in Figure 4.19.

There are many reasons the demand curve for money may shift. When a government issues bonds and increases spending, the demand curve may shift to the right.

WHY SUPPLY AND DEMAND OF MONEY WILL NOT AUTOMATICALLY REACH THE OPTIMAL INTEREST RATE

In a free capital market, the interest rate is determined by the supply curve and the demand curve. Because the supply curve is less sensitive to the interest rate changes, the capital market is not a fully functioning market. In other words, sometimes, the supply curve does not respond to a change in the interest rate. In this situation only the demand curve determines the interest rate.

Secondly, today most governments use a central bank to control the interest rate of their economy. In the U.S. the Federal Reserve Board meets periodically to decide the interest rate in an attempt to bring and keep inflation under control. During Asia's financial crisis in 1997 and 1998, Hong Kong, Thailand, Indonesia and other countries used interest rates as a way to control the flight of capital from their region or country. To many economists and governments, the interest rate is a multipurpose parameter that a government can adjust to achieve inflation control and capital market stabilization, as well as to stimulate the national economy, when needed.

For these reasons, the interest rate as manipulated by a central bank or government will rarely be equal to the optimal interest as defined in Chapter Three.

THE SURPLUS VALUE AND REAL PROFIT

When there is 10% inflation, and stocks earn at a 10% profit rate, the stock investment does not actually earn anything real, since inflation devalues the money.

real profit rate = nominal profit rate - inflation rate

Real profit could be surplus value, but it does not have to be surplus value. Real profit could contain no surplus value at all, or contain some surplus value, or contain only surplus value. The following will present the three different cases.

Consider a firm. Let us study its profits at three different times T1, T2, T3. One year is the interval between the three different times. During

Table 4.4

	T1	T2	T3
Monetary equivalent of one labor hour	$10	$12	$12
Input capital (labor hours)	500	500	500
Input labor (labor hour)	100	100	100

the period from T1 to T2, the inflation rate is 5% per year. The capital included in Table 4.4 is used capital, which refers to the capital that transferred to the final product.

The first period starts at T1 and ends at T2. If the investors invested 500 labor hours of capital at T1, how much should the investors get back at T2 as return? According to the equal exchange of value, the investors should get the same amount of labor hours in return. The value of 500 labor hours is equivalent to $5000 ($10 × 500) at T1, and $6000 ($12 × 500) at T2. Therefore, the profit rate is:

($6000 - $5000)/$5000 = 20%

The nominal profit rate is 20%. The real profit rate is 15% (subtracting 5% inflation rate from the nominal profit rate). Because the exchange is done according to equal exchange of value, there is no surplus value made by the investors. Thus, real profit may contain no surplus value.

However, if the investors get $6600 at T2 instead of $6000, there will be surplus value. (This occurs before the price of the product returns to the equilibrium point. See Chapter One.) In this case, the profit rate is:

($6600 - $5000)/$5000 = 32%

The nominal profit rate is 32% and the real profit rate will be 27% (subtracting 5% inflation rate). In this case, the real profit contains some surplus value, but not all is surplus value.

The second period starts at T2 and ends at T3. During this period, the investors invested 500 labor hours of capital. It is equivalent to $6000 at T1 and ($12 × 500 =) $6000 at T2. Suppose the total return to the investors at T2 is $6400, which is $400 more than what the investors should get according to the equal exchange of value. This $400 is the surplus value. The profit rate is:

6400/6000 - 1 = 6.66%

Suppose the inflation rate during this period is 2%, then the real profit rate is 4.66%. The real profit in this case is all surplus value.

While Marx believed profit is a form of surplus value, our analysis shows that real profit may contain no surplus value, some surplus value, or only surplus value.

MARKET CLASSIFICATION

Market classification is based on the conditions that are necessary for the market to function. Below is a list of conditions required for a market to function. If a market cannot meet one or more of these conditions, the market is not functioning perfectly. A human intervention (that is, government intervention) may be necessary to bring the market to function.

1. Some people in the market are motivated by their own material interests. They want to gain as much as possible in the exchange of goods at market. Overall, people are selfish.
2. Each market participant can switch from one trade to the other, such as switching from producing beef to pork. People are free to enter into production and leave production. Producers are free to decide what to produce, at what quantity, at what quality, how to produce, where to produce, and when to produce.
3. Goods must be reproducible. (Non-reproducible goods do not have perfect market characteristics.)
4. Producers are free to decide at what price to sell, where to sell, when to sell, and what quantity to sell.
5. There are many producers in the market for each kind of product so that no single producer can manipulate the price of goods on the market. There is no monopoly or oligopoly. It is a fully competitive market.
6. There is a free flow of factors of production, such as labor, material, information, capital, knowledge, and technology. Producers have information about other producers.

When a commodity in concern meets all of the above conditions, the commodity market is considered a fully functional market, perfect competitive market, or perfect market. In the real world, many commodities are in an environment that cannot meet all the above conditions. The markets of those commodities are considered to be dysfunctional markets. By applying the above conditions, we can tell which markets are functional, and which are dysfunctional.

PARADOXES

In the following several examples, I will illustrate some paradoxes and provide explanations as to when a market is functioning, and when it will be dysfunctional.

What is the major difference between a fully functional market and a dysfunctional market? In the dysfunctional market, the price of the commodity will not move toward the labor value needed to reproduce it, while in the fully functional market, the price of commodity will move toward the equilibrium where the price reflects the labor value necessary to produce or reproduce it.

PARADOX 1 (DIAMOND)

Several centuries ago, after one day of hard work in the corn field, a farmer walked back to his home. As he walked, he saw a shining stone in the field, and picked it up and examined it. It was a diamond. He took the stone to a market and sold it for 20 ounces of gold. This diamond which cost him no labor was equal in value to years of his farming. One year of hard labor in the corn field would only be able to be exchanged for a fraction of the diamond's value. If the labor theory of value was correct, how can it be that a diamond which took no labor to obtain has so much value, while the farmer's long hours of hard labor were worth so little?

The diamond story does not meet requirement 3, which says that "the goods must be reproducible." Neither does it meet requirement 5, which states that "there are many producers in the market for each kind of product so that no single producer can manipulate the price of goods at market." According to the new labor theory of value, only in the perfect competitive market will the equilibrium point of exchange be equal to the labor value necessary to reproduce the goods. In a non-perfect market, the equilibrium of exchange value may not be equal to the labor value necessary to produce the goods.

First, the commodity, a diamond was not reproducible several centuries ago. Diamonds then were obtained by pure luck, by discovery.

Since the diamond cannot be reproduced, its supply is limited. Even when the price is very high, no producers were able to produce diamonds for profit. Since no producer can profit from the high price of diamonds, the price of the diamond will not fall to the labor value necessary to produce it. The supply and demand curve is shown in Figure 4.20. The supply curve S1 is straight up because the price increase does not cause the supplied quantity of diamond to increase. Since the demand for diamonds is responsive to the price of the diamond, thus the demand curve goes down from the upper left corner of the graph to the right.

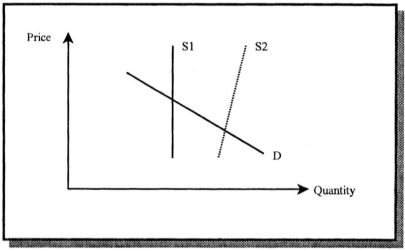

Figure 4.20   Supply and Demand Curve for Diamond

        Second, as mining technology improves, companies start producing diamonds from mines. However, only a limited number of mines are found to produce diamonds. The production of diamonds is still in a monopoly or oligopoly. However, the supply of diamonds may still be limited in comparison with the demand. In such a situation, the supply curve slightly goes up as the price increases. (See the dotted supply curve S2 in Figure 4.20) The demand curve goes down as the price drops, and more quantity is demanded.

        Third, the price of goods is equal to the value of goods only when the price is at equilibrium. We are not sure if the above diamond paradox depicts an equilibrium scenario. Furthermore, the value of the commodity is determined by the socially necessary labor to produce it, not a particular labor. If the diamond industry produced 99.99% of the world diamonds, and the other 0.01% of diamonds were picked up by the farmers depicted in the above story, and if it takes the diamond industry 100 labor hours to produce one diamond, and farmers no labor to obtain 0.01% of diamond supplied at the market, the value of the diamond can be estimated as below:

$$(100 \text{ labor hours} \times 99.99\% + 0 \times 0.01\%)/100\%$$
$$= 99.99 \text{ labor hours}$$

The value of the diamond is 99.99 labor hours instead of zero hour. This is because the value of a commodity is determined not by a particular producer or supplier, but by the socially necessary labor hours. The word "socially" means average of all suppliers and producers at the market.

PARADOX 2 (PAPER CURRENCY)

If Marx's labor theory of value is correct, that the value of good is determined by the average labor hours it contains, why does paper money, which contains so few labor hours, have so much value?

Paper currency does not meet requirements 2 and 5 for a perfect competitive market. Therefore, the price of the paper currency will not move toward the labor value necessary to produce it. Condition 2 states that "each market participant can switch from one trade to another, such as switching from producing beef to pork. People are free to enter into and leave production. Producers are free to decide what to produce, at what quantity, at what quality, how to produce, where to produce, and when to produce." Condition 5 states that "there are many producers in the market for each kind of product so that no single producer can manipulate the price of goods at market. There is no monopoly or oligopoly. It is a fully competitive market."

Currency or paper money is a special commodity. The supply of this commodity is monopolized by the government or government-authorized central bank of an economy. In other words, the value of the paper currency is created due to the limited supply of the paper money. Since paper money is not in itself a fully functional market, the value of paper money will not drop to the labor value necessary to produce the paper money. This is shown by Figure 4.21.

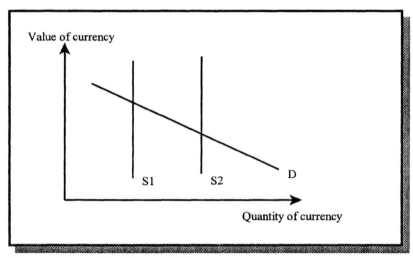

Figure 4.21   The Value of Currency

In Figure 4.21, Curve D is the demand curve for currency. The vertical line S1 and S2 represent two supply curves of currency, which is controlled by the government. As the government decides to increase the money supply, the curve shifts to the right from S1 to S2. When the value of the money decreases, there may be inflation.

PARADOX 3 (OLD WINE)

According to Marx's labor theory of value, the exchange value is determined by the labor necessary to produce the goods. If exchange value of goods is determined by the labor value, then how can old wine have a much higher exchange value than fresh wine? When wine is produced, the labor needed to produce it is fixed into the product. Simply keeping the wine for several decades should not increase the exchange value of the wine, according to Marx's labor theory of value. Yet, the reality is that old wine can sell for as much as 100 times the original price.

This old wine story does not meet condition 3, which states, "Goods must be reproducible." Therefore, the price of the older wine will not be moved toward the labor value necessary to reproduce it.

According to this theory, as presented in Chapter One, the reason that the new wine price is different from the old wine price is because the market for old wine is not a fully functional market. Old wine is not reproducible. No one can produce even one kilogram of 20-year-old wine today. If this year the market for old wine is extremely good, producers would want to make a huge profit by making more bottles of

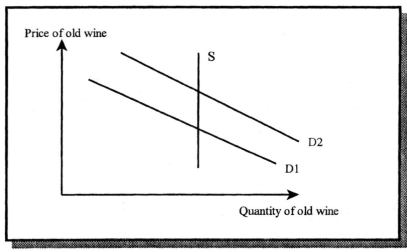

Figure 4.22   Supply and Demand for Old Wine

20-year-old-wine today. Can anyone do it? No, no one can produce old wine today. Old wine can only be produced in the past (i.e., 20 years ago). The second reason is that the price per average socially necessary labor hour is changing. For example, while it may have cost $1 to hire an average labor hour 20 years ago, today it may cost $5 to hire that same average labor hour. Thus, even the same bottle of wine that used one labor hour to produce will cost $5 per bottle today, while it cost only $1 twenty years ago. As the technology advances, the production cost of wine decreases. It is very likely it cost more average labor hours to produce the same wine 20 years ago than it does today. For these reasons, the price of old wine would be higher than that of new wine, even if the old wine could be made reproducible. Figure 4.22 illustrates the wine price in the supply and demand relationship.

The curve S is the supply curve in Figure 4.22. It is vertical because the supply of old wine cannot be increased. Curve D1 and D2 represent two demand curves. When demand shifts either from D1 to D2 or from D2 to D1, the price of the old wine changes.

PARADOX 4 (WATER IN THE DESERT)

At a river side, a cup of water may be worth little or nothing at all. However, it is worth a lot of money to a thirsty traveler in the desert. Some economists claim that the exchange value is determined by marginal value. Water costs less near a river because there is plenty of water. Therefore, the marginal utility of water is very low. In the desert, water is scarce, so it will be worth more, since the marginal utility of the water increases as the total available water decreases. Therefore, the value of goods is not determined by the labor used to produce or reproduce them. It is instead determined by marginal utility.

This story does not meet the perfect competitive market Conditions 3 and 5. Therefore, the price of the commodity will not move toward the labor value needed to reproduce the goods. Condition 3 states that "Goods must be reproducible." (Nonreproducible goods do not have the perfect market characteristics.) Condition 5 states that "there are many producers in the market for each kind of product so that no single producer can manipulate the price of goods at market. There is no monopoly or oligopoly. It is a fully competitive market." The supply and demand curves are similar to those in Figure 4.22.

Consider the following reversed case. Suppose a River Authority has legal claim to the river. Because there is only one river nearby, the River Authority decides to sell the water at a higher price. A cup of water at the riverside is sold for $4.00. Because there is no competition and thirsty travelers have money to pay for it, the River Authority is able to make a nice profit. A traveler, Kathy, has three bottles of water for one day near the river where water is plenty. The next day, Kathy travels into a desert as part of her tourist trip. She only has $1 left in her pocket. There are many bottled-water sellers waiting there since the tourist forecast predicted a huge crowd. But most of the tourists do not arrive due to bad weather. Thirsty Kathy is able to bargain with a bottled-water seller to buy a bottle of water at $1. However, she has to live on this one bottle of water for one day. Therefore, I can cautiously conclude that the higher the marginal utility, the lower the price; and the lower the marginal utility, the higher the price. In the desert the marginal utility of water is higher since Kathy has only one bottle per day, but Kathy only paid $1 for a bottle of water. In comparison to the riverside, the marginal utility is lower since she has three bottles per day, but the price of a bottle of water is higher. It is higher than Kathy pays when she is in the desert. Thus, marginal utility is a "good" tool to explain exchange value, but the marginal utility theory should be restated as following: the price of a commodity has an inverse relation to the marginal utility of the commodity. The higher the marginal utility, the lower the price; the lower the marginal utility, the higher the price. (Funny isn't it?)

PARADOX 5 (SCARCE COMMODITY)

Many rare commodities command inconceivably high prices at marketplaces, such as old postal stamps, rare books, coins, artwork, or antiques. The prices that people are willing to pay for scarce commodity are much higher than the labor needed to produce or reproduce them. Thus, it is the marginal utility that determines the exchange value.

This story does not meet perfect competitive market Conditions 3 and 5. Therefore, the price of the commodities will not move toward the labor value needed to reproduce the goods. Condition 3 states that "Goods must be reproducible." (Non-reproducible goods do not have the perfect market characteristics.) Condition 5 states that "there are many producers in the market for each kind of product so that no single producer can manipulate the price of goods at market. There is no monopoly or oligopoly. It is a fully competitive market." The supply and demand curves of rare commodities are similar to those in Figure 4.22.

PARADOX 6 (LAND MARKET)

If the labor theory of value is correct, why is the price of land not zero? Land as we know it does not contain any labor; rather, it exists on earth through no human intervention. If it does not contain any labor value, it should cost nothing on the market, and no one should have to pay for a piece of land.

The land market is not a fully functional market. As we discussed earlier, only in a fully functional market will the price of the commodity be forced by market mechanisms to move toward the price level that correctly reflects the necessary labor to reproduce it. Land, as we know, cannot be reproduced. Although technological advances in construction engineering allow us to build high-rise buildings, people still cannot reproduce land for any specific location. Land is not reproducible. Therefore, the supply of land is limited. When demand for land increases, the price of land will increase. This is similar to what depicted in Figure 4.22.

This story does not meet perfect competitive market Conditions 3 and 5. The supply and demand curves are similar to those in Figure 4.22.

APPLICATION EXAMPLES

EXAMPLE 4.4

Suppose a company Z has nominal profit rates as shown in Table 4.5. The inflation rate of the economy is also included in the table. The real profit rate in Table 4.5 is calculated by subtracting the inflation rate from the nominal profit rate.

Table 4.5

Year	1995	1998
Nominal profit rate	11%	8%
Inflation rate	5%	3%
Real profit rate	6%	5%

When we look at the real profit rate in Table 4.5, we know that Z Company had a better year in 1995 than in 1998. We want to know how Z Company is performing compared with the average real profit rate of the economy.

From Chapter Three, we have $P + 1 = (1 + S)(1 + I) - \Delta$. Suppose we have the following S and I data for the economy. We use S and I to calculate the P in this equation, assume $\Delta = 0$. Then, we use P minus inflation rate to compute the real profit rate (Table 4.6).

Table 4.6

Year	1995	1998
I	5%	3%
S	8%	1%
P	13.4%	4.03%
Real Profit	8.4%	1.03%

The average real profit of the economy is 8.4% for 1995, and 1.03% for 1998. Comparing these with Z Company's real profit, we find that in 1995 Z Company's performance of 6% was below the average real profit 8.4% of the economy. While in 1998 Z Company's performance of 5% was higher than the average real profit 1.03% of the economy.

EXAMPLE 4.5

A central bank of a country wants to set the interest rate. We can use the following equation from Chapter Three:
$R = L$
Suppose the economy $L = 3\%$. How much should the interest rate be? The central bank should set the interest rate at 3%, according to the above equation.

EXAMPLE 4.6

Suppose an economy has a productivity growth rate $S = 7.8\%$, and inflation rate $I = -2\%$. What can we predict about the average nominal profit rate of the economy? We can use this equation from Chapter Two for the ideal economy.

$$P + 1 = (1 + S)(1 + I)$$
$$P = 5.644\%$$

We can predict according to the above estimate that the average nominal profit rate will be 5.644%. The real profit rate will equal 7.644% (Real profit rate = Nominal profit rate - inflation rate). Because the real economy has unemployment, the nominal profit rate tends to be higher than the P calculated by using the equation for ideal economy. Thus, the average nominal profit rate of the economy is perhaps 1 to 2% higher than 5.644% estimated by the equation. So the answer is the average nominal profit rate of the economy is about 6 - 7%.

EXAMPLE 4.7

Suppose an economy has a 7% average nominal profit rate, while the average compensation for the labor force increases 5%. What can we know about the economy? Use this equation:

$$L + 1 = P + 1$$

From this equation we know that the average nominal profit rate of the economy should be equal to the labor force compensation increase. A perfect competitive market with full employment is very close to the ideal economy. If the economy has a perfect competitive market with full employment, L should be roughly equal to P. When L < P, we know the economy is either not experiencing full employment or is not a perfect competitive market.

EXAMPLE 4.8

Suppose an economy experiences an 8% GDP growth in a year while the inflation is 5%. Assume we can treat it as an ideal economy. However, the steel industry has an average profit rate of only 2% while the average price of steel has not changed over the year. What can we say about the steel industry?

When the total workforce change is negligible, the GDP growth rate can be used as the productivity growth rate for the economy. So we have S = 8% and inflation rate I = 5%. Using the equation

$$P + 1 = (1 + S)(1 + I)$$
$$P = 13.4\%$$

The average profit rate of the economy should be equal to 13.4%

while the steel industry has only a 2% average profit rate. This suggests that the steel industry have overproduced steel. It is very likely that the capacity utilization is relatively low. Using the following equation from Chapter Two:

$(C + 1)(1 + B) = 1 + P$

The price change rate of steel $C = 0$. We can estimate the productivity growth rate of the steel industry B.

$B = P = 13.4\%$

At equilibrium, the steel industry should have an average profit rate of 13.4% and a productivity growth rate of 13.4%. Since, the steel industry only has a 2% profit rate, we can infer that the steel industry only made a 2% productivity improvement.

SUMMARY OF CONCLUSIONS

1.   A managed market economy is more desirable than a free market economy. A free market economy is not desirable, and is actually no longer in practice. The task of economics is to provide guidance for economic management.

2.   Consumers make purchase decisions by intuition and feeling. A commodity may produce satisfaction for a consumer even without being used as intended, or even purchased.

3.   Although on average consumers are trying to maximize their satisfaction, the reality is that consumers may not be able to reach the theoretical maximum utility. Consumer utility maximization is often impossible given limited resources for decision-making. These limited resources include time, money, knowledge, human resources, and information.

4.   Finding a proper level of decision-making is very difficult if not impossible. The utility maximization of an individual, business, or government cannot be achieved with 100% certainty.

5.   The mainstream exchange theory (marginalist exchange theory) is wrong. Marginal utility cannot be equal to price as a general case due to the budget constraint. As a result, marginal utility cannot be used to explain the exchange value.

6.   The theory of price and theory of value have partially intersecting domains.

7.   Under a perfect competitive market without inflation and productivity improvement, when the price of a commodity experiences a bell-shaped movement, there is a demand curve shift to the right. The consumption level increases during the same time period. When the price of a commodity experiences a reversed bell-curve movement, the demand curve has shifted to the left. The consumption level decreases during the same time period.

8.   An ideal economy must also be a perfect competitive market. The perfect market may or may not be an ideal economy.

9.   The supply curve of money is often less sensitive to the interest rate change. Under some economic conditions, the supply curve of money is a vertical line for the concerned interest rate range.

10.   The market does not move the interest rate, the profit rate, and the

compensation increase rate for labor hours toward the optimal interest rate, optimal profit rate, and optimal compensation increase rate. Therefore, government intervention to bring these economic parameters close to optimal parameters may be necessary to improve economic efficiency.

11. Eventually all investment options will have the same marginal return, as investors move money from less profitable investment vehicles to more profitable investment vehicles.

12. Real profit may contain no surplus value, some surplus value, or only surplus value.

13. When the commodity in question meets all 6 conditions discussed in this chapter, the commodity market is considered a fully functional market, perfect competitive market, or perfect market. In the real world, many commodity markets cannot meet all of the above conditions. The markets of those commodities are considered to be dysfunctional markets. In dysfunctional markets, the price of the commodity will not move toward the socially necessary labor needed to produce the commodity.

THE LAWS OF ECONOMICS

THE LAW OF PERFECT MARKETS

Equal exchange value is the rule for perfect markets. The value of a commodity is determined by the socially necessary labor to reproduce it. When two goods change hands at equilibrium, they exchange with equal value. Since both the buyer and seller want the best and most profitable exchange, they will only agree to exchange goods at the point where the buyer's payment and seller's goods have the same value. When goods are exchanged according to the law of equal exchange of value, economic resources can be optimally allocated.

Under perfect competitive market conditions, at equilibrium, the exchange happens at an equal exchange of value.

THE LAW OF IDEAL ECONOMY

An economy can operate at its peak economic efficiency only if goods are exchanged by the rule of equal exchange of value. The word "goods" refers to things involved with exchange, such as capital, labor, money, and services.

When an economy is operating at its peak economic efficiency, the economic parameters will have the following relations:

$$V(1) = V(0)(1 + S)(1 + I)$$
$$[V(1) - V(0)]/V(0) + 1$$
$$= R + 1$$
$$= L + 1$$
$$= P + 1$$
$$=(C + 1)(1 + B)$$
$$= (1 + S)(1 + I)$$

Where:

       C: price change rate for the product

S: productivity growth rate of the economy
B: productivity growth rate of a business, or an industry
I: inflation rate of the economy (consumer goods and services)
L: labor monetary compensation increase rate
R: interest rate
P: profit rate of a business or industry
V(1):   monetary equivalent of one labor hour at the end of period
V(0):   monetary equivalent of one labor hour at the beginning of the period

THE LAW OF OPTIMAL PARAMETERS FOR REAL WORLD ECONOMY

$$V(1) = V(0)[(1 + S)(1 + I) - \Delta$$
$$(1 + C)(1 + B) = (1 + S)(1 + I) - \Delta$$
$$1 + R = (1 + S)(1 + I) - \Delta$$
$$1 + P = (1 + S)(1 + I) - \Delta$$
$$1 + L = (1 + S)(1 + I) - \Delta$$

Where:

Δ: wage compensator
C: price change rate for the product
S: productivity growth rate of the economy
B: productivity growth rate of a business, or an industry
I: inflation rate of the economy (consumer goods and services)
L: labor monetary compensation increase rate
R: interest rate (nominal interest rate)
P: profit rate of a business or industry, or the average profit rate of the economy (nominal profit rate)
V(1):   monetary equivalent of one labor hour at the end of the period
V(0):   monetary equivalent of one labor hour at the beginning of the period

REFERENCES

METHODOLOGY

Barry Barnes: "T.S. Kuhn and Social Science," 1982.

Charles Michael Andres Clark: "Economic Theory and Natural Philosophy: The Search for Natural Laws of Economy," 1992.

Daniel M. Hausman: "The Philosophy of Economics."

Mark Blaug: "The Methodology of Economics," Cambridge Univesity Press, 1980.

Mark Skousen: "Economics on Trial," IRWIN Professional Publishing, 1991.

Philip Gasper, and J.D. Trout: "The Philosophy of Science," MIT Press, 1995.

Roger E. Backhouse (Editor): "New Directions in Economic Methodology (Economics As Social Theory)," 1994.

Subroto Roy: "Philosophy of Economics," Chapman and Hall, Inc., New York, 1991.

HISTORY OF ECONOMIC THINKING

Christopher D. MacKie: "Canonizing Economic Theory: How Theories and Ideas Are Selected in Economics,"1998.

David L. Prychitko (editor): "Why Economists Disagree," State

University of New York Press, 1998.

Ernesto Screpanti and Stefano Zamagni: "An Outline of the History of Economic Thought," Oxford University Press Inc., New York, 1995.

Karl Pribram: "A History of Economic Reasoning," The Johns Hopkins University Press, Baltimore, 1986.

Maurice Herbert, Dobb: "Theories of Value and Distribution Since Adam Smith: Ideology and Economic Theory," Cambridge University Press, 1975.

Todd G. Buchholz: "New Ideas From Dead Economists," Penguin Books USA Inc., New York, 1990.

W. W. Rostow: "Theorists of Economic Growth From David Hume to the Present," Oxford University Press, 1990.

Lionel Robbins: " A History of Economic Thought," Princeton University Press, New Jersey, 1998.

ECONOMIC THEORY

Adam Smith: "An Inquiry Into the Nature and Causes of the Wealth of Nations," Liberty Classics, Indianapolis, 1979.

David Ricardo: "On The Principles of Political Economy and Taxation," London: John Murray, Albemarle-Street, 1817 (third edition 1821).

Jack Hirshleifer: "Price Theory and Applications," Prentice Hall College Division, 1997.

John Maynard Keynes: "The General Theory of Employment, Interest, and Money," Prometheus Books, New York, 1997.

Karl Marx: "Capital," Penguin Books, 1976.

W Stanley Jevons: "The Theory of Political Economy,"Macmillan and Co., London, 1879.

A collection of classic economic theories can be found at website: Melbecon.unimelb.edu.au

ECONOMIC HISTORY

Jeremy Atack: "A New Economic View of American History," W.W. Norton & Company, 1994.

TEXTBOOK

David R. Kamerschen, Richard B. McKenzie, Clark Nardinelli: "Economics," Houghton Mifflin Company, 1989.

James D. Gwartney, Richard L. Stroup: "Economics," Harcourt Brace Jovanovich, Inc. 1987.

Ralph T. Byrns, Gerald W. Stone: "Economics," Harper Collins Publishers, New York, 1992.

Roger N. Waud: "Economics," Harper & Row, Publishers, New York, 1989.

William J. Baumol, Alan S. Blinder: "Economics," Harcourt Brace Jovanovich, Publishers, 1988.

William Boyes, Michael Melvin: "Economics," Houghton Mifflin Company, 1991.

ABOUT THE AUTHOR

Stephan H. Loh is a theoretical economist. He began studying economics right after he graduated from Beijing University of Aeronautics and Astronauts, China, in 1982, with a Bachelor of Science in Electronic Telecommunication Engineering. He taught himself economics and started looking for educational opportunities in the U.S. In 1986, he was admitted to Southern Oregon State University. In 1988, he graduated with a Master of Science in Business Administration. To pursue his dream of becoming a professional economist, he studied economics in a masters program at Indiana State University in 1989. In 1990, he transferred to The Johns Hopkins University to pursue a Ph.D. in economics with financial help from Eileen and Auther Lin. Unable to make sense of mainstream economics, he quit university studies in 1992. He continues his study of economics with his own innovative approach.

Do you want to know the answers to the following questions?

Questions	Answer
Why did U.S. economy have a higher productivity growth rate (3.19%) in the 1960s than 1990s (1.01%)?	Page 172
How should a central bank set the interest rate for an economy?	Page 175
At what rate will my college tuition increase?	Page 85
What is wrong with marginalist value theory?	Pages 101,186, 216
How do you explain the paradoxes that challenge the labor theory of value?	Page 216
According to Karl Marx, all profit is surplus value. Is Marx right?	Page 214
If a country adopts this theory, it is expected that the productivity growth rate could be 2% higher in the long run.	Page 172
How do you estimate the productivity growth rate for an industry?	Page 145,158
How do you evaluate the performance of a business?	Page 207, 224
Do you have any further Research topics I can write a paper on?	Page 204
How do you estimate price change?	Page 206

Learn how to improve the productivity growth rate for an economy as much as 216%.

Explain why the U.S. economy had a higher productivity growth rate in the 1960s than 1990s.

The most important economic theory of the 20th century.

What every economist should read.

What every economic student should read.

A revolution in economic thinking.

What every economic policy maker should read.

RET